7.95

55p

Books by James Herndon

Notes from a Schoolteacher

James Herndon

SIMON AND SCHUSTER

NEW YORK

Copyright © 1985 by James Herndon
All rights reserved
including the right of reproduction
in whole or in part in any form
Published by Simon and Schuster
A Division of Simon & Schuster, Inc.
Simon & Schuster Building
Rockefeller Center
1230 Avenue of the Americas
New York, New York 10020

SIMON AND SCHUSTER and colophon are registered trademarks of
Simon & Schuster, Inc.
Designed by Irving Perkins Associates
Manufactured in the United States of America
10 9 8 7 6 5 4 3 2

Library of Congress Cataloging in Publication Data
Herndon, James, date.
   Notes from a schoolteacher.

   1. Education, Secondary—California—San Francisco
Metropolitan Area—Case studies.   2. Junior high schools—
California—San Francisco Metropolitan Area—Case studies.
I. Title.
LA245.S4H47   1985   373.794′61   85-8298
ISBN: 0-671-54371-7

   The author is grateful for permission to reprint from *A Wave* by
John Ashbery. © 1984 by John Ashbery. Reprinted by permission of
Viking Penguin, Inc.

For Raoul Teilhet

Contents

8

Is it enough
That the dish of milk is set out at night?
   —JOHN ASHBERY

Prologue: The Fountain

*Experience is never categorical; what matters
about it is always detailed and personal.*
—EDGAR FRIEDENBERG

Last Friday, June 17, was the last day of school for this year
at old Spanish Main Junior High.

We teachers were not doing much. The seventh graders
were gone. Yesterday was their last day and they had gotten
their report cards and cleaned out their lockers and gone
home early, in the usual hubbub of exchanges with teachers,
wherein our most aggravating students told us that we were
the best teachers they had ever had and we told our favorite
students that we were shipping them off to the Falkland Islands or somewhere, to which they answered, Thank God! or
some such—all of this according to a code developed and
understood by teachers and students for a hundred years.

The eighth graders were up at the high school, enduring
graduation practice with the principal, vice-principal, counselor, several duty-bound eighth-grade teachers, and the band.
We all knew what would happen there. The kids, although

11

dying to graduate and look right and to have everything go right and having spent money on hairdos and clothes and gotten tickets to the graduation for parents and grandparents and uncles and all, would be refusing to shut up and pay attention while the principal was trying to tell them what to do, since they had already practiced two days in a row here at Spanish Main and figured they *knew* what to do, although displaying right then absolutely no evidence that they did, and the principal's frustration would catch up with him and lots of yelling and shouted orders would go on, until mercifully the time would be up and the buses would carry everyone back in various kinds of bad moods.

We knew all that. We sat in the teachers' room, talking, having coffee, and occasionally got up and went out to clean out our rooms, or turn in our First Aid Kit or our Grade Book or the *Tierra Firma District Curriculum Guide,* or to try to get the librarian to sign us out with our Library Inventory—all the important things which needed to be done and signed for if we were to be able to end the year, get our checks . . .

We made plans to go to lunch. The kids, once back, would be freed at 12:01. We could go out to lunch then, although we'd have to come back to get our checks. When? Three-ten, the usual time we leave on a regular day. We check each other out. Three-ten? That's what He said. *He* is, of course, the principal. We have other names for Him on occasion, none flattering as to brains, competency, or style. *He* seems to work best for everyday usage. No, the union can't do anything about it. As usual, we protest to each other that it is unreasonable and unnecessary. There is nothing for us to do here. Besides that, there are only two or three days in the year when we get to go *out* to lunch, a long lunch together, drinking martinis and such and eating something other than our cottage cheese, fruit yogurt, sandwiches, or the school hamburgers. We look forward to it, we plan to be very jolly, but we do not want to come back.

This turns our thoughts, inevitably, to the subject of Him and principals in general. We begin to make a pool on the time He will actually give out the checks. We speculate; will it be ten minutes early? Right at 3:10? Half an hour early? We know He wants to remain the boss, even—*especially*—on this last day when we might be tempted to take liberties, but we also figure He'll try to be a good guy too. But just how much good guy and still remain *boss?* We know that is going through his mind. Of course, if graduation practice was worse than usual, He'll be grimmer than usual, and that is a factor.

Ever since—perhaps ten years ago, or twelve? fifteen?—principals began to be called "middle-management" and we teachers became "FTE's" (Full-Time Employees), we had seen these guys—men and women—struggling to be our buddies while still maintaining a suitable distance in order to be *management*. Being "a part of the staff" is, of course, no longer considered. It is a very difficult path to tread, and very few have ever been able to do it. Still, being "good guy," on occasion, is part of "management technique"; we teachers know that there is an administrative handbook telling principals how to do this—what ratio of good guy to boss—although we have never seen it. Even those of us with administrative credentials have never seen it. It must be given out only after one actually becomes management.

Actually, the up-and-coming term is *Program Manager*.

We got the pool lined up, beginning at 2:45 and ending at 3:10, each minute, a dollar a throw. We decided to wait until the rest of us came back from graduation practice to finish it off. We began to laugh a lot; we regarded the pool as an act of sabotage. We knew He would hear about it, sometime during the afternoon. We also realized that, as an act of sabotage, it was, at best, minor-league. We're a pretty miserable lot, we told each other, if that's the best we can do! Still, we weren't seriously depressed. We understand, tacitly, that in order to really cause Him trouble, we would have to cause trouble for the school itself; we aren't willing to do that, somehow. So we laughed again about what a sorry bunch we were, but we were pleased with ourselves anyway.

There began to be remarks about other, earlier, middle-management ne'er-do-wells. We are a staff which has been together, for the most part, for quite a few years. Those new to Spanish Main are not new to Tierra Firma School District, but are mostly former elementary-school teachers who, for one reason or the other, decided to brave the wilds of junior high. They told us again about principals they had worked with, for, or under, depending . . . and we brought up the succession of principals at Spanish Main and we remembered and reestablished the principle, developed a hundred years ago by teachers, to wit: *do not attempt to rid yourself of your principal, no matter how bad you think he may be. They have another, much worse, waiting in the wings!*

These are last-day thoughts, not Spanish Main thoughts. Not unique. After all, there are fourteen more schools right here in Tierra Firma alone, all enduring the last day of school with its burden of a year's cares and troubles, each with its own Him, or, it may be, Her . . .

Ten o'clock. We had another two hours with nothing much to do. There is no question that we are feeling the tensions, the upsets, the aggravations of the last days of school; today's questions add to it. We occasionally broke out of the teachers' room and journeyed out into the school, looking it over. I went to my room, Room 33. The thirty-six desks were shoved over to the side to make it ready for the summer cleaning crew. I opened the cabinets where the books had been put away, and immediately wished that they had been put away in a more orderly fashion. I remembered, too, that that thought had crossed my mind while we were putting them away. I believed it crossed my mind every year for the last twenty or so years.

The only thing I had left to do in order to sign out and get

my check and say *adios* for this season was to put in a Work
Order for things that needed fixing. The darkening curtain
was ripped in seven places. That was what Andy had told
me, a day or two before. He counted the rips. Rent, I told
Andy. The curtain is *rent*. No reason to say that, I just felt
like it. It just barely worked for showing movies—educational films, I mean (remembering years back when it was
verboten to say "movies")—but it really looked bad. "Get
that curtain sewed up, Mr. Herndon!" kids are always saying.
"Boy, it's really ugly!"

Sew up darkening curtain, I wrote on my Work Order. The
room has a high ceiling and the wall to the northeast is all
window. You can see the Tierra Firma Shopping Center and
a good deal of the rest of the place and, ten miles beyond,
much of the city, including the Miro-like TV tower, near
which I live.

"Where do you live, Mr. Herndon?" kids ask every day.
"See that tower?" I ask. Everyone abandons work to take a
look at the tower. I fall for it every time. *"That's* where I
live!" Quite a few kids then fall to arguing about whether I
really live in, on, or about that tower.

I believe I'm babbling. Well, it's the last day of the year,
the season. I bet ballplayers babble in the same way. Just outside the room is a strip of grass about twenty feet wide, running the length of the school. It's a very pleasant room, I
think to myself. The grass is full of gopher mounds and next
to one of them a black-and-white cat is sitting patiently, waiting for a gopher to come out. Cats have sat there the last two
or three—four? five? ten?—years, I reflect. We—students and
I—have never seen them catch a gopher. God knows we have
watched. The cats must come from the apartments right below the school. We can see into the apartment windows, at
least those on the upper story, and girls are always claiming
that some naked, *perverted* man is showing off in the windows.

The grass strip is actually, now, a strip of foot-and-a-half-high dandelions, quite pretty, the result of a squabble between school board members about the gardening contract.

See, there was this old Tierra Firma outfit, a hometown Italian company, which did the gardening for the district for years and years. "I do it at a loss!" cried the old man at school board meetings. "At a loss! Just to do my part for the town and for the schools and for the kids! Because I live here!"

But a couple of new members were elected to the school board, to whom anything connected with the old board and the superintendent was suspect, and they hired a new gardening company for a quarter of the amount, thus saving money for "educational needs," which naturally couldn't be argued with, but as it happened the new gardener was from another town, *across the Bay!* and was black, too, so then somehow the old guard got together and payment to the new gardener was blocked on the ground he wasn't doing the job, so of course, he stopped cutting the grass . . .

I know all this because, as union president (Local 3267, American Federation of Teachers, AFL-CIO, I'll just mention), I go to all the board meetings, and one thing you can see there, or you remember there, is that there really *was* an old Tierra Firma, a railroad-head cowtown before the city was anything much; then later a town of small farmers and greenhouses which supplied the city and the peninsula with cut flowers . . . and, of course, for the last thirty years there has been the new Tierra Firma with row on row of developer houses with backyards on curving streets, those houses once making a millionaire of Malvina Reynolds for the song "Little Boxes"; and that these two sides do not always get along.

Now the gardener from across the bay knows that too. Still, years after Malvina, many of these same houses and streets look quite charming as I drive to work. The houses are the same—oh, maybe a den or an extra bedroom added on—but trees have grown up, flowers and vines grow and blossom wonderfully in the foggy weather and, in fact, little remains of the plastic look which one had predicted could only get worse.

The above musing is not getting me out of here with my check. There is always a certain anxiety generated in a teacher on the last day, in particular. You have this damn slip of paper, dittoed off, upon which you must obtain signatures for doing right. The fact that you have been able to do so for, say, twenty years, does not help. Things may have changed this year without notice. I realize I'm not done with Work Order.

Fix Drinking Fountain, I write on it. Now that's it for the Work Order. When I moved into this room four—five? six? seven?—years ago, the fountain didn't work. So I'm used to writing in *Fix Drinking Fountain.* Last summer it actually did get fixed, but after a month or so some kid stuffed ground-up crayons down its throat, which caused it, when turned on, to squirt a nice stream of water fifteen feet across the room into the laps and essays of students, who all screamed happily and who then had to be let out of the room to the bathroom to dry off because their shoes or jackets or pants or skirts were new or because they had just gotten over the flu anyway and couldn't risk pneumonia or who got to stand up angrily and swear that there was *no way* they were copying this ruined work over, usually crumpling up the wet work so that no investigation of it by me would be possible . . .

No worry about time lines here. This particular squirting fountain was this year. My own reaction was normal. I put up with it all one day, got a wrench from the shop teacher after school, and turned it off. That act was discovered by the very first kid who came into my first-period class. He knew it was turned off before he even tried it. We are used to that clairvoyance in school.

There followed, all day long, students trooping up to me to tell on old Andy. I already knew Andy did it. We all did.

I didn't see Andy do it, and I doubt they did. Well, maybe some of them did. We all knew anyway. Andy did it.

I took it all as occasion for a *Discussion*. It went much better than most of my lecture/discussions, because the subject was important. The kids' question was, "When are you turning the water back on?" Everyone paid attention. It was Learning.

"Never!" I said.

"Well how are we going to drink water then?"

"I don't know," I said, "and I don't care. I don't want a drink."

"Well, we do!"

I shrug. By this time I have everyone's attention, every class, all day, and realize without any guilt at all that I am beginning to have a good time. Everyone, for once, listens to me. I point out that I didn't sabotage the fountain.

"Andy did!" they cry, selling him out, also without any qualm at all. Andy is sitting right there.

They know the score. I am to punish Andy and then, justice being served, turn the water back on. I ain't going to kill Andy, after all. Andy says nothing. They fire on, full of suggestions; now the discussion, they figure, is over. Michael (the custodian) will fix it. Call Maintenance!

Well, you can see how the rest of it goes. I didn't sabotage the fountain, I repeat, and neither did Michael and neither did Maintenance, and furthermore neither of them need to drink water from this fountain. (*But we do!*) So when *you* fix it so it doesn't squirt out fifteen feet anymore, I'll turn it back on! We have approached a stalemate.

Teachers don't win many stalemated negotiations, in my experience, but I have the upper hand in this one. Some kids fool with the fountain for the next few days, without result, and some can be heard exhorting Andy to fix it, or they'll have to take action. They point out (I can hear them, although officially paying no attention) that he, Andy, has acted against their own welfare. The fountain is important in their school lives; when they can't stand to sit there one moment longer, even the best students can say to themselves, I'm just going to get a drink! They get to get up, walk, move—just for a second. It is often enough.

They point this out to Andy.

"Mr. Herndon"—(I hear them saying)—"don't care! Come on, Andy!" Nothing at all happens, though, because Andy will not move at all, and because everyone in the class *likes* Andy, troublesome or not, including me.

There is quite a bit of commentary in the media (once again!) about Education, which, I guess, is nice to see. Is the above Learning? Education? No, I think not, although in the late sixties many of us thought it was, or at least that this kind of discussion had something to do with morals, the world, real-life, responsibility, *Existenz* . . . no one *learned* anything from the above, because we already knew all about it to begin with. What we were doing was *pointing out* to each other, once again, for the thousandth time, what the score was, the rule, the point, the upshot of things . . . a lesson, in itself maybe valuable, certainly interesting, perhaps crucial, and unquestionably fun for all.

Pointing out. The papers, the media, the new state superintendent (of California), the (California) Round Table of Concerned Businessmen, well, *fuck them,* I begin to think, perhaps a little pointing out might be just the thing, maybe they could use a little . . . hold it! I tell myself, let's get the hell out of here first.

Take a last look at the room, looks OK, turn the key, and gone. Gone for only a little while, sure; come back next year and see about it once again.

Of course, for all my teacher power, the kids won in the end. Having no water to drink available in the classroom, the result of my hard-hearted stance, they had to go out to drink water, out into the halls. But generally, the halls are forbidden during class time. We can't have all these rascals roaming the halls, causing trouble. Now, to my lucky students, I've added another *real* reason to go out and roam—we have to drink water!

I'm quite annoyed, but it's not entirely about the fountain; the kids know I'll let them out to "drink water" (and that I'll forbid it too, once in a while, for no reason; I just feel like it!) and so that's fine and we get to enjoy the pretense that I am hard-hearted and tight.

No, what I'm unaccountably annoyed by is this phrase "go drink water," which, I see, I've now written a few times. That's what the *cholo* kids say when they want to go get a drink of water. They say, "Mr. Herndon, can I (often, "May I") go drink water?" These damn girls—I have it in mind that it is always *girls*—come up to me and say, "May I go drink water?"

It hits me every time. They all write and read English, spell fine, many do good and get good grades, but—whether they were born in the city or in Nicaragua or El Salvador or Peru—I want them to say, May I go get a drink! Spozed to go that way. Can I go get a drink! Not this May I go drink water! . . . I never bring it up, of course, but it drives me crazy. I'm no different, I tell myself, from all the old-lady Italian teachers in the city who used to bitch about bilingual classes, saying, *My* parents never spoke English, *I* had to learn English to survive, so why in hell can't *they?*

Cholos. When I was growing up in L.A., if you ever said the word *cholo* when some actual *cholos* were around, you were in for real trouble. Now, *cholos* describe themselves proudly as *cholos.* Now that points out . . .

Later for the *cholos.* I have things to do. I go down to the main office and turn in my Work Order and get my sheet signed by the secretary. I scan the sheet; everything is signed for except the library and the principal (room in order). He is up at the high school trying to get the students to practice. I head for the library.

Usually the librarian—actually the library aide—gives you

an inventory sheet of all the books you ought to have and you take it, have someone (not Andy!) count up how many books you actually have, and then, since you never have the right amount, you invent how many to put under Lost, Missing, or Discarded. I never had any trouble with that.

But this year, there is no inventory. We are supposed to make out our own list! I'm annoyed again—how come everyone gets to stop doing their job except us, the teachers?

Well, this year the board cut the library aide's hours in half, in response to the superintendent's recommendation to cut out the librarian *and* the clerk (which is what he recommends every year). So that's why. . . Still, the union went to bat for the librarian's job and the clerk's and in fact claims some credit for their reinstatement and so teachers shouldn't have to do their job, and indeed (as may already be clear) I haven't done my own inventory and it's too late now . . .

Anyway, the librarian isn't there. She's up at graduation practice. How come? *He* made her go, says the clerk.

But never mind. Yesterday the seventh graders had to scurry around to make sure their lockers were cleaned out, to make sure they found lost jackets, found or paid for or told plausible lies about lost books and P.E. locks in order to get checked out so that they could get their report cards.

On my way back to the faculty room, I run into Harold. Harold is also scurrying around. He asks me if I've seen the librarian. Now I know that Harold has every book accounted for since the beginning of time, that he has none lost, strayed, or stolen. Still, he's anxious. He has only been teaching school for thirty-five years, more than twenty of them here. Besides that, he is quitting. Retiring. This is it! he told me, swearing me at the same time to silence. He doesn't want anyone to know. No retirement parties, no gold watch, he says. Still, everyone knows. That's OK with Harold too, so long as no one says anything to him about it. At the same time, he's worried about getting his ditto sheet signed.

In the teacher's room, we speculate about when they'll get

back from graduation practice. We want the pool filled up. We are quite gay; a cameraderie is present which we rarely have and we indeed love it. The mention of graduation, however, encourages some to speak with a certain bitterness.

First, there was the promise that really bad, worthless students would not be allowed to graduate from the stage. As we speak, we all feel that it is silly and fear we may sound vindictive. Actually, we *are* feeling vindictive for the moment and may have felt so for the past—oh, three weeks, as the season ran down.

I put everything I had on the line for that little asshole! (this is the kind of thing we say today)—tried to show him he *could* do it if he just *would* do it and by God he could, he did! I saw it! and gave him all the leeway I could in the world and when that didn't work got tough and kept him after to do his work—and he can do it, goddammit! sure, if he was just plain dumb, then OK, OK! but he's not . . . had his parents in, they'll straighten him out! of course! and then suddenly it's the last month of school and it's still the same old horseshit and Hey! I realize I've got the rest of this class, probably most of them not as smart as he is, trying their best and I've probably neglected them and so I finally say to myself, Well, to hell with you, kid! and I talk to Him and He says *these kids* can't be allowed to graduate from the stage . . .

Change. We all read, every day now in the papers, hear every day on the TV, about change in the schools, reforms, higher standards of discipline, incompetent teachers, more money. The above will show you the only change I'm aware of—we teachers now curse a lot, openly. Five—six? seven?—years ago I first heard an extremely respected and respectable woman teacher come into the faculty room and say loudly, Shit! and then, after a pause, *and double-shit!* That was a signpost, an icebreaker, and since then we all, male and female, respected and respectable or not, feel free to say "bullshit" and "asshole." That does not appear to be the change the media are talking about.

We're a bit beaten down. We're all ready to say the same thing—to wit, we don't give a damn if the worst student in the school graduates from the stage. Just say so—fine with us. Everyone graduates! They're all going up to high school anyway, whether they officially graduate or not.

That's our official stand, true or not. But we can't stand it that we get "standards" agreed upon, in fact, laid on us without any real consultation anyway, and so we lay these standards on the kids and in the end the standards are thrown out the window and the kids say, *You see?*

We say it too, here in the faculty room, with an hour left to go until noon.

Well, someone says, *He* says that many of these kids aren't going to finish high school anyway, and so this will be their last chance to graduate with their parents watching and . . . *Fine!* we interrupt. Fine with us! Then just say so at the outset! We don't need this hypocritical bullshit! We don't need this club over the kids. We can handle them, even if He can't. All we need is just, one time, a simple statement of policy which turns out to be true.

Anyway, says Joe, He told someone up at the office that the reason we have graduation at night up at the high school is because *His Teachers* want it that way!

This is a bombshell. What? *What?* He said what? . . . who told you . . . heard it from . . . and the school secretary . . . that's the way all information comes to us in the district—anyway, that's what He said.

We all hate that. We hate everything about it. First of all, we don't want to be *His Teachers*. We don't want the kids to graduate up at the high school at night. It's too pretentious, it forces the parents to spend too much money, and most of the parents don't have much money.

We don't get to see the kids dressed up and graduating,

which we've always liked. The kids always graduated nicely in folding chairs out on the blacktop, the parents sat in more folding chairs, it never rained once in twenty years, and by noon it was over and done with and was quite OK, nice, even. That's how we've always done it, until this . . .

We don't get to see it because we're not going up there at night, on principle! His first year, He held a faculty meeting to discuss graduating at the high school at night. The faculty voted against it, unanimously. The result was that we held it at night, and that He stopped consulting us. That first graduation, the superintendent called me up and said he was surprised to hear that no teachers showed up for graduation. I told him it was because we'd been asked our opinion, voted against it and that, since we couldn't be made to go, we didn't go.

As time went on, some teachers showed up at graduation, voluntarily, out of a sense of—well, what? Responsibility to the kids, seemed to be it. Some of us feel these teachers are selling us out. If no one ever showed up, we say, He'd have to knock it off with these damn graduations. Maybe not though, others argue. A whole litany of exasperation follows. After all, He thinks it's *His* school, *His* students, *His* parents, *His* teachers, *His* buildings, *His* diplomas . . . and it's damn sure *His* graduation! Well, then let Him do it!

There are eight or ten of us here in the teachers' room. We sit around tables with coffee, sit at certain tables at which, with few exceptions, we have sat all year, perhaps for several years. We are more of a solid group today than we usually are. Now someone laughs. It is Maggie.

No point in all this, she says. It's not like it's anything new.

We are reminded that these same subjects come up on this last day every year. They are exactly the same. Nothing has ever been done about them. It's safe to say nothing ever will, or can, be done about them. Nothing will, or can, be done about almost everything that really drives us crazy in our lives as teachers. No matter how we perceive the school, no matter what we think about how the education of junior high students should go, no matter what we think about how to deal with the students who don't make it in our school, or the kids that do make it—and our opinions on these subjects are anything but unanimous—we know that nothing real will ever be done to change or even ameliorate these conditions. They are permanent.

Still, we go on talking about them for a bit; it is the last day. We bring up all of our discontents, perhaps just to take a look at them. We mention textbooks, sillier every year, more expensive, cheaply bound so that they fall apart. We speculate on next year's schedule of classes, which for the last three years has appeared before us on opening day so entirely screwed up that it took five weeks of changing kids and entire classes around before school was even operable—*His* schedule, we of course point out, not forgetting to add that if we made lesson plans like that schedule, we would be, and should have been, fired on the spot. We bring up supplies (never have any) and class sizes (way too large, or why is it that one class with thirty-six students sits right next door to another, same grade and subject, with twenty-three?) and the utility (or the reverse) of Chapter I, Title This-and-That, ESL and bilingual education, trying to remember what exactly each is about or for. We bring up reforms and our own exhaustion.

A little silence takes over, as the above list provides us with a sinking sensation. We combat it, each silent and alone. It takes more than that to defeat us completely though; we are pros. We're all thinking the same thing, making our comebacks.

We are the team here. Whatever is done here, we do it. We make the plays, we hit the ball, or no one does. So the manager claims it's *His* club—the owner says, "*My* club!" It ain't their club at all. Now we can look back and see that we had respectable seasons; had a reasonably low ERA, hit for a decent average, with not a few clutch hits. Made the plays most of the time. We begin to remember some good days.

"You know what I really like about the last couple of weeks?" Clementine says it. Her tone changes our mood at once. She's going to say something we all feel and that we all like. Something *true* that we'll all like to hear. Someone always does.

It's when I can forget my lesson plan, forget worrying about homework coming in or not, when I know I've done my best, good or bad, who knows? done all I can do and I can just let go and play and talk with the kids I really like. I have a pretty good time then. You know, we never get a chance, not the whole year long, to really talk with the students, just talk about things, without worrying about the rest of the class, about discipline, are they getting the lesson? . . .

Ho man, that's so true! Everyone is affected by that. The room breaks up into individual conversations for a bit as teachers tell other teachers about so-and-so and so-and-so who are great kids and what they said and what we said. We are all happy as larks, singing a cheerful tune.

Indeed, before the last two weeks began, up came Mark and Juliette and Melinda and checked my grade book and inquired as to their own grades and chattered about nothing much until finally the question came out, approached sideways as if of no great importance, What if we didn't do this last week's assignment? Would we still get an A? Yes.

That being agreed to, we can spend the last two weeks in pleasant and profitable conversation, rewarded as we are, quite properly, for having done right all year.

The rest of the class is split into two groups. There are ne'er-do-wells who have awakened to the fact that they are going to have to take report cards home shortly and suddenly wish to escape retribution. They now want to do "extra-credit" work. For them, after an appropriate amount of lecturing, pointing out how they got themselves into this fix (along with the irony of doing "extra-credit" while having neglected to do the "regular" assignments)—I produce a number of ditto sheets which they now actually begin grinding out, huddled together with the dictionary, atlas, and the textbook, *working*, planning to take home a C instead of a D minus.

Another smaller group of real, antischool hardliners are occupied with "cleaning up." It is their turn to do right. Andy is supervising the careful taking down of papers from the walls, passing them back to their authors if present, the cleaning out of desks, the removal of staples, and the orderly putting away of books. Andy has not exactly volunteered for this work; he simply *informed* me that he was going to organize this activity. It is not his fault that I now wish the books had been put away in a more orderly fashion. Andy would have done it and made others do it. It is I who haven't the will, these last two weeks. A certain amount of disorder is produced at first, between Andy and Charmaine, who wants to help but only if she is boss. I am pretty slick at this kind of thing by now, though, and send Charmaine outside on important errands. Given no direction by me, Andy has had the books arranged in stacks according to size, which makes the stacks look very neat.

Actually, the entire aspect of class has changed. I'm only thinking of one particular class here, but it's the same with the rest of the day.

Andy and his group of antischool demonstrators have become desirable workers. They want to do what they are doing, and can see the benefit, the virtue, of their work. They are not concerned, it seems, with report cards. Andy lets me know that I should have let him take care of the classroom all year long. He implies some disdain for my ideas of order, even my capability for such order.

Yeah, but I can't, I couldn't, Andy, because you're supposed to be doing your schoolwork first, and you never did it.

Andy shrugs. He can't get through to me, can't make me understand, his shrug says. We both forget about the fountain. How's the room looking? he asks. Fine, Andy, fine! I tell him. Andy is from Peru. He reads well. His writing is fine, his English fine. His "skills" are fine. Could we start over? Well, clearly not.

But anyway, the real bad guys are doing solid work. The repentent ne'er-do-wells are slaving over the ditto sheets. Say, Mr. Herndon, says Mark, who has been roaming the room overseeing the latter effort, don't you think those ditto sheets are kind of meaningless?

He goes on to explain, not meaning any insult, I mean, we had that stuff all year!

Well, OK, Mark, but these guys haven't done that stuff all year.

Well, yeah. Mark is unconvinced. He reminds me that we never had ditto sheets all year. We had to write *essays*.

I remind him of the change in circumstances; it is the last two weeks.

Juliette is Indian, by way of Africa and Fiji. How can anyone just sit here all year and do nothing? she wants to know, talking about the ditto-sheet workers. I mean, it's so *boring!*

Well, what are you doing right now? I say. You're just sitting around doing nothing. If you're so bored, start doing the ditto sheets. Who was it asked me if they could forget about schoolwork this week? Are you bored?

See, Juliette! says Melinda. Melinda is Chinese. Mark is Polish. Yeah, Juliette! he says. They go off together to discuss this new insight. They roam around, stopped continually by workers to give out answers to questions which cannot be immediately found in dictionary or atlas. Soon they will be back to bait me, without any fear of retribution. We are comrades.

In the faculty room, I think about it, the last two weeks, the change in the class. It's pretty good. I remind myself that it's only in a social studies class that this picture can exist, at least among "academic" classes, since it is the only class that is not "tracked"—that is, schoolboys, averages, and no-goods are all thrown in together. In English, reading, and math the schoolboys are all thrown together, the no-goods all together, under the pretense that . . . well, that's another subject, also nothing new.

I'm jerked out of this reverie by a phone call.

It's Jerry, the vice-principal at one of the other junior highs. (There are three, containing seventh and eighth graders; the district has twelve elementary schools. Well, one of the junior highs became a middle school a few years back, containing sixth, seventh, and eighth graders, perhaps just so the district could have a middle school when they came into fashion.) Jerry has a problem with the union. He has a job opening at his school, a teacher he wants to put in that job, and the teacher wants the job. Now he hears that the union won't let him do it.

"What the hell's going on here?" he wants to know.

Jerry and I are pretty good friends. He used to be the vice-principal at Spanish Main and worked hard and did a good job and also made out the football pool with a friend of his—in short, a good, smart guy. The principal at his school is retiring and he might get the job; we all hope so, although some among us believe that his very competency may disqualify him.

Look, he tells me, I think Adele is the best person for the job, she's taken courses for it, signed up to take more courses this summer, I ought to be able to put her on and she ought to be able to get the job. What's wrong with that?

I explain, not for the first time. It's the contract. It says, Jerry, that if there is a new position created by the board, then it has to be advertised, *posted* in all the schools, so people have the opportunity to apply. So then they apply, and then you interview them, and the best one gets the job. Simple.

Jerry complains that it ends up just being a matter of seniority, who gets the job, and that's what's wrong with it. I realize his problem—namely, that another teacher from the school wants the job too, and has more seniority than Adele.

Not so, I say. Seniority only decides when the two candidates are equal in every other way. You get to do the interviewing and get to have your say, and by and large your say counts a lot, unless you do something really capricious.

Capricious is a very useful word for the union. I remind Jerry that he brought all this trouble on himself. He told Adele she could have the job. She told everyone else; all this before any other teacher even knew there was such a job opening. Liz, the other teacher who wants the job, was properly pissed off. She, unlike the other two, *had* read the contract, and called me in order to ask me why she ought to pay dues to a union that couldn't enforce its own contract.

Naturally, I said that we could, and would. I explained it to Adele, who also pays dues (and wondered why the union didn't want her to have the job she wanted, was qualified for, etc.). I blamed it all on Jerry, as I now tell him.

If you'll just follow procedures, you'll get good teachers, in the long run. I advise him to call Roy, the personnel director, and get Roy to post the damn job, and he says OK, he understands it and he will.

I tell him, Look, Jerry, the reason we put stuff like that in the contract is that for years principals have abused the hiring of teachers, hired their sycophants whether they were best for the job or not, transferred people out of their school because they didn't kiss ass, ran the school as though it was their own little country club, and that he, Jerry, ought to know that . . .

Yeah, yeah, I get it, he said, but I still think Adele's best for the job because . . .

OK, Jerry, I say, that's what you say after the interview, if you still think so. Meantime, call Roy.

I get off the phone. Back in the teachers' room, people look at me inquiringly. Maybe I just heard something important, like who would be principal at Spanish Main next year.

Or, the board had laid off five administrative positions last week—maybe I'd heard who would get the ax; these same speculations also traditional on the last day, year after year.

I told Peggy, who is a friend of Adele's, what Jerry had said, and what I had said. I planned to call Liz later on. Peggy said it would still be a shame if Adele didn't get the job, since she was going to get her M.A. in computer literacy and was best for the job. I said Liz had taken courses too, and that anyway the point was we had to follow procedures and she said she understood that. You know, I said, it's probably OK if it's Jerry doing the choosing, since he's both competent and fair, but what if it's . . . ?

Everyone is listening; it's clear that we all understand that.

The bus comes back from the high school. The kids are turned loose and the teachers come in. They are worn out, and show signs of great exasperation. How did it go? we ask them.

It's the same old story. *He* stands up there lecturing the kids and telling them to quiet down—and listen to Him—and they don't quiet down and He keeps lecturing on—how in the world can He keep on talking when no one's listening? For God's sake!

Every year, we all say, including those of us who have never been to graduation practice. How long has He been principal? Four? five? Seven years . . . ?

Gary enters.

I want everybody's attention! he says loudly. Unlike the kids, we pay attention.

Gary teaches P.E. and math and supervises in the lunch-time cafeteria. He is chief among those of us who feel that there should be clear rules about transgressions, and that these rules should be carried out. They seldom are, of course. When he comes into the teachers' room, it is often to report some new outrage. We are always ready to hear it.

I just want everyone to hear this from the horse's mouth, he says, before you hear it from anybody else!

He tells his story. First of all, he was not pleased to be ordered to go up to graduation practice. He wasn't in line to go up there; now, all of a sudden, it's an order.

So, OK, Gary says. I'm sitting there reading my *Time* magazine. I don't have a group, I'm not responsible for anything there, have no duties, there is no reason for me to be there! So I'm reading *Time*.

The next thing I know, there *He* is, bending over—get this, I mean He's *bending down* so His face is level with mine—and He shouts out, Stand up!

Stand up? Well, I snap out of *Time* and look at Him, I mean, I'm astonished, I can't *believe* this man! and then I realize the band is practicing "The Star Spangled Banner" and He wants me to stand up for it. Without even thinking about it, I shout back, No!

So what happened then? we all want to know. Well, He just kind of backed off and I continued to read *Time,* except now of course I wasn't reading it . . . so nothing happened. But you'll all have to hear about it, I know, so I'm just telling you my version to begin with.

The other point is, says Gary, I just don't get up, for either the flag or the song. I stopped doing that quite some time ago. Never mind why, but I did. Stopped.

We all wait a bit for Him to come in, or do something. We can count on Him being really upset. We figure that since the kids wouldn't pay attention, He had to give some kind of order to a teacher, to show He was still the boss. Obviously that hadn't worked out.

He ought to have had sense enough, at least, to pick someone a little more docile, or someone who didn't give a damn. It was predictable, though, that He did not. Still, He didn't come in, and shortly after that most of us went out to lunch.

· · ·

We're quite jolly at lunch. We can take as long as we like, a couple of hours at least; we are free. We have drinks, mention summer plans, make guesses about next year's principals, about what time will win today's pool, about what He will do about Gary. We agree He can't do a damn thing. We're not certain He knows that. We wonder about money from the state for a raise in salary next year.

In the end, we talk about those of us leaving this year. Two women have already left, in the middle of the year, their years of night-school courses in accounting and real estate having paid off. (That made Him angry too, we remember, since it left a hole in His school and because they did not consult Him first about their futures.) Another teacher is leaving on account of disability. Joe is taking a leave of absence in order to study, officially, but we all figure he has another job, another *kind* of job, taking a leave just in case it doesn't work out. I'm going to work part-time next year.

Harold is leaving. We all realize the school will not be the same without Harold. Someone brings up the fact that the two women who quit are making less money to start and working much longer hours and are happy as hell about it.

At least here you're treated as an adult, Amy said, says a friend of Amy's.

I think that Harold is my age, almost exactly, and has had it with schoolteaching. Still, I haven't been teaching for thirty-five years; yeah, only twenty-three, I tell myself. I remind myself to say, somewhere, that people shouldn't start in teaching school just out of college but ought to do something else for a while, maybe for fifteen years. Otherwise, they never see anything *but* school and it assumes too much importance, as if it's the whole world. Now, if the school likes to be taken as a microcosm, a bush-league metaphor for the real world, that's fine with me, and it certainly does often seem as if that is what it is, but it is not the whole world . . .

but Harold does stand for something like the old days, to be sure. He has his own system for teaching reading and English and social studies and it does not vary much, not because Harold is not creative or competent or whatever it currently is that teachers are not, but because he worked it out a long time ago and it suits his style and that's the way he does it. We get the idea from kids that he talks, they listen—listen to stories about growing up on the farm in North Dakota, the Germans, the Irish, who lived there, the nuns in school, the Indians, mixed in with stories about ancient Egypt and Marathon and Michelangelo—I realize that I don't know just how Harold's room works, because you don't just go into Harold's room to see what he's up to. Harold closes the door, and inside it's his own little universe. Microcosm.

Actually, that's true of most of us. The thing is, Harold seems to us now as the last of the old-fashioned schoolteachers, dressing every day in a different suit and tie, a storyteller, a wit, and a moralist. We will not see his like in Spanish Main again.

We talk some at lunch about the bad press we currently get. Our conclusion, in brief, is that if anyone thinks the trouble with public schools comes from incompetent teachers, they are crazy as hell. We figure that before you get around to the teachers, you'd better investigate the incompetent administrators, the crazy parents, society, dope, standardized testing, Sony Walkmans, the economy and the job market, ex-Governor Jerry Brown, TV, rock-and-roll, nuclear weapons, racism and sexism, and Vietnam, to name a few, not necessarily in that order.

Incompetent teachers? I think. When haven't we been? Or, incompetent at what? There is no such thing as teaching school competently.

Back at school, full of food and drink, both unaccustomed at this time of day, we wait. I try the librarian, but the library door is locked; knocking gets no response. This check-out still isn't settled and I feel even less like doing it than before. I get back and the phone rings for me. It's Jerry again.

He tells me that Roy says that he can't post the job because the board hasn't officially approved it yet, so there is no job, even though there is. Also, he says, even if they did approve it, they couldn't have interviews for it, since the principal has to be in on the interview and the board hasn't decided yet who will be the principal here and so . . .

Right, I say. To myself I say, They'll do all this during the summer when no teachers are around and hope to do as they please. I advise Jerry to call Dave, the superintendent, and get him to get the board to approve the job anyway. Jerry reminds me that Dave and some board members are at odds these days, so that probably won't do any good.

Well, anyway, thanks, he says. I have some idea about what's going on, at least.

I remind him that he hasn't got any computers anyway, to go with his new computer literacy course and teacher. The board approved the computers, but not the money for them, because some board members are mad at the computer company over the maintenance bill.

Hell, says Jerry. No way I'm going to worry about this anymore. I'm just going home and look at the ocean. Anyway, how do I know I'll even have this job next year? I might be right back in the classroom! Somebody will be, that's for damn sure!

Right, Jerry, I say. Fate worse than death!

All administrators, even the best ones, talk about "going back to the classroom" as something to be hated and feared. What the hell do they think *we* do? What do they think a school district is all about? The classroom, that's what it's all about!

Well. I call Liz. She takes it surprisingly well. It's not life or death if I get the computer job, she says, although it would be nice to try something new. If I don't get it, I could take the science job at your school, now that Amy's gone. But

I'm damn tired of being fucked over, excuse the language, and if there was one good thing I thought the union had done, it was to establish fair transfer procedures, and so when I heard this I got mad again—anyway, I'm glad everything is straightened out. That's all I ask. Keep up the good work!

That pleased me enough so that when He came grimly up and said He wanted to see me in His office, I didn't mind. By God, we *do* have a good policy, and it makes life fairer and better!

So what's up? I said.

He was pacing, very red, more angry than I'd seen Him in some time. He told me that, by God, it was a damn shame He was going to have to reprimand some teacher on the last day, He didn't like to have unpleasantness the last day, but by God He was going to have to do it! He looked at me, to see if I knew what it was about.

He's talking about Gary, I guess. I'm also aware that this same guy has done something unpleasant *every* last day since He's been here. He particularly likes to pick out some teacher and say, while handing out the check, I don't think I'll have a place for you next year!

I can't let this go by, Jim! Here I spend the whole year trying to teach my students to respect the flag in my school and then one of My Teachers—look, what kind of model is that! I sign his check, dammit, and that just—well, it's *betraying* me, that's what it is!

I'm surprised at that. Teach the kids to stand up for the flag? When was that? We don't do the flag salute in school anymore, haven't for years. Not since Dave was principal here and ordered everyone to salute the flag in class, but then discovered we didn't have any flags, so *bought* flags and even came into my room to lead the salute, or to make sure I was doing it, it's hard to tell, but forgot how it went halfway through . . .

Well, I say, it's your right to call him in, and his right to have me here as representative, but you know all that. You can call him in. But when you call him in, what are you going to do about it?

I don't mention the fact that He doesn't pay Gary's salary, that the same guy signs Gary's check as signs His. It's an old sore point with the faculty. Why do you insist on saying you sign our checks? Bob asked him once in faculty meeting. Here's my check! waving it around in a fit of exasperation, Is this your signature?

Well, I've got to do something. I won't be able to sleep this weekend if I don't do something! It's an insult! He tells me.

OK, OK, I say, but I'm still asking you what are you going to do when you get him in here?

I'm trying to be reasonable in my role of union rep, a kind of teacher shop steward. I'm remembering too that He has a right to tell Gary to go up to the High School during working hours, if He wants, but if He didn't have anything for Gary to do there, we could argue that it was *capricious*. I also know that He is one of the few principals who has read the contract and abides by it, at least the letter, if not the spirit. Still, He's furious. Gary didn't obey.

Look, I say. You know no one has to stand up for the flag if they don't want to. I see you didn't like it, but you know Gary is just going to tell you he doesn't stand up for the flag. What do you say then? It's going to be So you don't like it? So what?

You won't like that either, I add.

He paces some more, and tells me He'll let me know later. On the way out, I wonder what difference this will make to the check pool. I've got 2:46, which doesn't look too good now.

I look for Gary, to tell him what happened. He's not to be found. I try the librarian again; no dice. When I get back to the teachers' room, He's just come in with his box of checks. He sits at a table, saying nothing, still looking grim. Someone checks the clock; three o'clock on the nose! Everyone moans except Bud, who goes over and collects the seventeen bucks.

He looks startled; this won't help His weekend, I guess. But at least, or so it turns out, He has forgotten all about the ditto sheets to be signed, a first in living memory, and hands out the checks, mine included.

Now I'm anxious to get out of there, in case He should remember the sign-out sheets; also, I'm tired of this day. Peggy, however, wants to bring up the computer literacy course. We have sixteen computers which presently act just like workbooks, printing out drills in math and reading. Many of us argue that especially with our students, meaning all our students who don't know much English (nor apparently much Spanish or Tagalog either), this is just what's needed. Short, intense bursts, three times a week, that's part of the reason our scores are up. (My scores, He says.)

The district has a computer committee, she reminds me, which has already stated that computer literacy as a requirement for all students is crazy! So why have the committee, if they're not going to pay any attention to it?

We agree that "comp lit," as it's already being called, means no drills for the ESL and slower kids. It also means fewer students for the other electives: homemaking, shop, art, music, foreign language.

I remind her that comp lit hasn't been approved by the board yet anyway. We make a plan to monitor board meetings and get teachers there to make speeches, should the subject come up. That'll be in the summer, she reminds me, and no one will be around . . . and so . . .

No. No more for now. You can see that, on this particular last day of school, just about every issue that is a part of schools and schoolteaching has been available for inspection. It is not that we or you, Readers, learn anything from it. There is nothing to learn here. Like my students and the fountain, we have all known it all along. This last day is no different than any other last day.

But we'll point it out. If presidents and presidential candidates are going to run for office on the basis that public schools are no good, and if they are going to suggest solutions to this surprising (and novel) problem, solutions ranging from more money to firing teachers who can't spell, from longer school hours and more homework to cutting out tenure (solutions, one must point out, neither surprising nor novel), *then*—then it ought to be pointed out, to everyone in this country who knows exactly what schools are and have always been, just what a school is.

As for us? We make promises to get together over the summer, and head for home.

PART I

A School Kit

*We were all down there at Mercer
University in Macon, Georgia, listening to some man tell us about
the use of Behavior Modification in
educating children in the classroom.
Edgar Friedenberg had sat there,
looking puzzled, for some time, but
suddenly he brightened up, as if
he'd just got the idea, and told the
guy, "Oh! Now I understand!
You're not talking about a* child.
*You're talking about a child-*kit!"

CHAPTER

1

Discontent

Gentle Reader, there have been schools in America for quite some time, and it has always been very difficult for everyone to be satisfied with them.

Therefore, every once in a while a group of experts gets together and makes rules for how the schools should behave.* Just so, in 1893 a Committee of Ten which included five college presidents and whose chairman was Charles Eliot, president of Harvard University, issued a document which recommended that all high school students, regardless of whether or not they intended to go to college, should receive a liberal education; they ought to study English, foreign languages, mathematics, history, and science.

Twenty-five years later, times had changed. Another committee (for the Re-Organization of Secondary Education) had altogether different plans for the high schools. This committee was chaired by the state supervisor of high schools in

---

* Much of the historical information that follows I read most recently in *The Troubled Crusade*, by Diane Ravitch. Ravitch is, of course, not responsible for my argument.

Massachusetts and consisted of professors of education, high school principals, and one college president who had been a professor of education.

They issued a document called *The Cardinal Principles of Secondary Education* in 1918. These principles were to be (1) Health, (2) Command of "fundamental processes," (3) Worthy home membership, (4) Vocation, (5) Citizenship, (6) Worthy use of leisure, and (7) Ethical character. It is said that "fundamental processes" were left out of the original draft.

I myself imagine that both groups quoted Thomas Jefferson to support their views, since that is what everyone in America who has any views at all always ends up doing. Indeed, I'll do so myself: in 1786, Jefferson, in France, wrote a friend of his in Virginia, hoping that the state would pass a bill "for the diffusion of knowledge among the people. No other sure foundation can be devised for the preservation of freedom and happiness," he wrote, adding that he had seen the people of France remaining in the grip of "ignorance [and] superstition" which led directly to their oppression. "Preach, my dear sir," Jefferson wrote, "a crusade against ignorance. Establish and improve the law for educating the common people."

So that's all there is to it, and should settle the matter.

(Only a cynic would remember that the German who advised the Prussian Junkers to grant free public schooling to the common people, somewhere around that time, assured the Junkers that the schools would teach the kids—the future industrial workers—to be prompt and diligent, to get to work on time, not to have to go to the bathroom or "drink water" every five minutes, and that whatever else they learned, like reading, couldn't hurt because the same Junkers controlled what they read anyway. Indeed, around 1948 or so, when I was in college and read this kind of thing, an article in *Kenyon Review* by an esteemed New Critic and poet, something of a hero of mine at the time, wrote about a liter-

he above four are the main ingredients of the crusade,
none of them are discontented, in the way that Mr.
an, and so on, are talking about.

ssatisfaction, of course. Disappointment, OK. Worry,
. We have changed the terms here.

imagine that my first-grade teacher, Ms. Cain, was dis-
ied with me. Well, I was dissatisfied with her too. I imag-
that she said, indeed I had *evidence* that she said, Jimmy
smart enough kid, if he'd only shut up once in a while
listen to me! I thought, at the time, if ol' Ms. Cain would
shut up a while and stop calling up my mother and tell-
her that . . .

is not new. Nothing about it is new. What seems to
en is that there comes a day when everyone decides, once
, that everyone is discontented with American public
ols. How that decision is made is a mystery, but every
in a while, it is made. Usually such a decision is accom-
ed by "test scores," which are, naturally, down. Every
ctable newspaper and journal then drags out an article,
nted every ten years or so, about a teacher or two who
spell. A mother or two will be found who will claim
her child, recently graduated from high school, cannot
Captains of industry are quoted to the effect that if we
had a well-educated work force, we wouldn't be in the
omic fix we're in. Investigators are sent out to report on
apanese school system, since it seems to result in selling
of automobiles, thus must have provided a well-educated
force.

he question was, Who is discontented? All of a sudden
nswer is: everyone in America is discontented.

---

acy movement in Egypt. He indicated that those Egyptians
were going to be better off remaining illiterate, since all they
would be able to read was Farouk's newspaper which was full
of lies that they would believe, since they would believe, as
converts do, anything in print. In their illiterate state, the
critic thought, they believed nothing and were better off.)

Well, we can recognize the above two dissenting opinions
as cavils; they are out of the mainstream and neither could
quote Jefferson. Everyone else, from Charles Eliot to John
Dewey to Ichabod Crane, would agree with Jefferson.

Ah, Readers, that has not seemed to settle the matter.

Still, one must admit that the crusade against ignorance
goes on. We all agree with it, we support it, pay taxes for it,
talk to our children about it, want the best out of it, and indeed work sometimes within some of the institutions created
to wage the crusade. We would not dream of saying, "Well,
to hell with it!"

But since everyone (in the mainstream, on the right path,
in their right minds, all good citizens) believes in the crusade, it is reasonable to wonder about the source of the discontent about it. We have, after all, plenty of public
schools—certainly more, and in better shape, than old Jefferson had or maybe even dreamed about; more, perhaps, than
he even wanted.

There is no shortage of common people to go to them,
either.

The schools have taken on every problem, every task, every
reform at the heart of the matter of American civilization—
from literacy to child labor to segregation to Vietnam to dope
to sex and, if the schools' scores are low on these matters, no
other institutions in the country even showed up for the test.
Compulsory education has been legislated, at first in order
to make the poor parents let their kids out of the fields or the
shop to go to school so that they should not be ignorant and in
danger of being oppressed. We did this by quoting Jefferson.

Later, the law was used to make the kids themselves go to school instead of going out to work where they might make some money. Some people have called *this* oppression, although they may find it more difficult to find an appropriate statement to quote.

Given all that, we still have to deal with the fact that *if* Mr. Reagan and *if* most governors and *if* most politicians ran for office on the ground of discontent with the crusade, then there must be some discontent.

And *if* there appeared a National Committee for Excellence to make plans (once again!) for how the schools should behave, and *if* another National Institute (in this case, Carnegie) came out shortly afterward with another plan, equally prestigious, but totally different—then it *must be* that Americans are discontented with the schools.

Who is?

And what are they discontented about?

Well, certainly, all teachers are discontented. They have always been, quite rightly. Believe it or not, the main discontent of teachers is not about their pay. It's in there, of course, but that is true of everybody, so it doesn't count.

Are school administrators discontented? I think not. They have become *management*—upper management for the superintendent and assistant superintendent for curriculum and the assistant superintendent for business, let's say; and middle management for the horde of supervisors and for the principals. They have *irritations*, of course, but these are part of the ball game, and in the main they say, in chorus, Let's make the system work! Besides, nothing bad which happens at school really affects them; it may affect management's *image*, but that's not the same. Given that there are exceptions, it is not usually the bent of management to change the workshop. If it ain't producing, they have no trouble finding fault. That they are one of the main sources of discontent among teachers is obvious. Well, management is discontented about its pay, of course.

Parents? Well, clearly, some parents take th[e] of the crusade in order to send them to paro[chial] private schools, or to no school at all. Thos[e] however, cannot be numbered in the ranks tented. In fact, they are fairly content. Their or their philosophies, have enabled them to av[oid] Even so, their reasons for taking their optio[n] crusade rarely have to do with *learning*, if we cation as having to do with learning. The rea[son] to do with violence, racism (often the same th[ing]) and advantage. But the common people? Th[e par]ents? They clearly have *worries*. Worries are discontents. Should the public school teacher and say the kid is doing OK, then they do not The teachers are common people too, and so e[ach] stands each other—the kid will do OK in America, will not remain in the grip of ignor[ance] stition, and will not be oppressed either. Of the kid not be doing OK, then the teacher Look, the kid is not doing the work, talks to *izes* too much, and must straighten up. The parent agree that the kid must shape up. doesn't; the result is *worry*.

We all agree with Jefferson. I have friends their kids, as little kids, Go to school, be on ti[me] clean, and don't smart off. That is the comm[on] vice, and it should suffice, and does suffice, un[til] kids decide to quit the business.

Kids? Well, the kids in school, just like the school, are *dissatisfied*. If this joint would just or the other thing, or if they just wouldn't do the other thing, we'd be happy, they say. The day. We say it too. It is true that the kids wh[o] unhappy with the school, and who make the unhappy (and who cause the administrators to the system work!) never miss a day of the crusa[de] acy movement in Egypt. He indicated that those Egyptians were going to be better off remaining illiterate, since all they would be able to read was Farouk's newspaper which was full of lies that they would believe, since they would believe, as converts do, anything in print. In their illiterate state, the critic thought, they believed nothing and were better off.)

Well, we can recognize the above two dissenting opinions as cavils; they are out of the mainstream and neither could quote Jefferson. Everyone else, from Charles Eliot to John Dewey to Ichabod Crane, would agree with Jefferson.

Ah, Readers, that has not seemed to settle the matter.

Still, one must admit that the crusade against ignorance goes on. We all agree with it, we support it, pay taxes for it, talk to our children about it, want the best out of it, and indeed work sometimes within some of the institutions created to wage the crusade. We would not dream of saying, "Well, to hell with it!"

But since everyone (in the mainstream, on the right path, in their right minds, all good citizens) believes in the crusade, it is reasonable to wonder about the source of the discontent about it. We have, after all, plenty of public schools—certainly more, and in better shape, than old Jefferson had or maybe even dreamed about; more, perhaps, than he even wanted.

There is no shortage of common people to go to them, either.

The schools have taken on every problem, every task, every reform at the heart of the matter of American civilization— from literacy to child labor to segregation to Vietnam to dope to sex and, if the schools' scores are low on these matters, no other institutions in the country even showed up for the test. Compulsory education has been legislated, at first in order to make the poor parents let their kids out of the fields or the shop to go to school so that they should not be ignorant and in danger of being oppressed. We did this by quoting Jefferson.

Later, the law was used to make the kids themselves go to school instead of going out to work where they might make some money. Some people have called *this* oppression, although they may find it more difficult to find an appropriate statement to quote.

Given all that, we still have to deal with the fact that *if* Mr. Reagan and *if* most governors and *if* most politicians ran for office on the ground of discontent with the crusade, then there must be some discontent.

And *if* there appeared a National Committee for Excellence to make plans (once again!) for how the schools should behave, and *if* another National Institute (in this case, Carnegie) came out shortly afterward with another plan, equally prestigious, but totally different—then it *must be* that Americans are discontented with the schools.

Who is?

And what are they discontented about?

Well, certainly, all teachers are discontented. They have always been, quite rightly. Believe it or not, the main discontent of teachers is not about their pay. It's in there, of course, but that is true of everybody, so it doesn't count.

Are school administrators discontented? I think not. They have become *management*—upper management for the superintendent and assistant superintendent for curriculum and the assistant superintendent for business, let's say; and middle management for the horde of supervisors and for the principals. They have *irritations,* of course, but these are part of the ball game, and in the main they say, in chorus, Let's make the system work! Besides, nothing bad which happens at school really affects them; it may affect management's *image,* but that's not the same. Given that there are exceptions, it is not usually the bent of management to change the workshop. If it ain't producing, they have no trouble finding fault. That they are one of the main sources of discontent among teachers is obvious. Well, management is discontented about its pay, of course.

Parents? Well, clearly, some parents take their children out of the crusade in order to send them to parochial schools or private schools, or to no school at all. Those who do that, however, cannot be numbered in the ranks of the discontented. In fact, they are fairly content. Their circumstances, or their philosophies, have enabled them to avoid discontent. Even so, their reasons for taking their options against the crusade rarely have to do with *learning*, if we are to take education as having to do with learning. The reasons have more to do with violence, racism (often the same thing), discipline, and advantage. But the common people? The common parents? They clearly have *worries*. Worries are not the same as discontents. Should the public school teacher like their child and say the kid is doing OK, then they do not have to worry. The teachers are common people too, and so everyone understands each other—the kid will do OK in the country of America, will not remain in the grip of ignorance and superstition, and will not be oppressed either. Of course, should the kid not be doing OK, then the teacher has got to say, Look, the kid is not doing the work, talks too much, *socializes* too much, and must straighten up. The teacher and the parent agree that the kid must shape up. Often the kid doesn't; the result is *worry*.

We all agree with Jefferson. I have friends who all said to their kids, as little kids, Go to school, be on time, be neat and clean, and don't smart off. That is the common people's advice, and it should suffice, and does suffice, until the common kids decide to quit the business.

Kids? Well, the kids in school, just like the teachers in the school, are *dissatisfied*. If this joint would just do this, or that, or the other thing, or if they just wouldn't do this, or that, or the other thing, we'd be happy, they say. They say this every day. We say it too. It is true that the kids who are the most unhappy with the school, and who make the teachers most unhappy (and who cause the administrators to say, Let's make the system work!) never miss a day of the crusade.

The above four are the main ingredients of the crusade, and none of them are discontented, in the way that Mr. Reagan, and so on, are talking about.

Dissatisfaction, of course. Disappointment, OK. Worry, right. We have changed the terms here.

I imagine that my first-grade teacher, Ms. Cain, was dissatisfied with me. Well, I was dissatisfied with her too. I imagined that she said, indeed I had *evidence* that she said, Jimmy is a smart enough kid, if he'd only shut up once in a while and listen to me! I thought, at the time, if ol' Ms. Cain would just shut up a while and stop calling up my mother and telling her that . . .

It is not new. Nothing about it is new. What seems to happen is that there comes a day when everyone decides, once again, that everyone is discontented with American public schools. How that decision is made is a mystery, but every once in a while, it is made. Usually such a decision is accompanied by "test scores," which are, naturally, down. Every respectable newspaper and journal then drags out an article, reprinted every ten years or so, about a teacher or two who can't spell. A mother or two will be found who will claim that her child, recently graduated from high school, cannot read. Captains of industry are quoted to the effect that if we just had a well-educated work force, we wouldn't be in the economic fix we're in. Investigators are sent out to report on the Japanese school system, since it seems to result in selling lots of automobiles, thus must have provided a well-educated work force.

The question was, Who is discontented? All of a sudden the answer is: everyone in America is discontented.

2

So, of Course, Finally, I Did Turn the Water Fountain On

*What is most extraordinary about youth today
is that adults everywhere should be so worried
about it.*

—EDGAR FRIEDENBERG

I do think that it is junior high school students, twelve- and thirteen-year-olds, who qualify as being "youth." I once taught second graders in summer school, and it was clear that they were not "youth." I once taught high-schoolers up in the mountains, and they were not quite "youth" either. I have, at various times and in various places, taught graduate students in universities, and they certainly were not youth.

So, one day after school, I went and got the wrench again and turned on the water. Of course, it was still plugged up. Still, Alex Rashed, an Arab kid who, born in the Argentine, considered himself to be a *cholo,* had just recently probed at it and guaranteed he would fix it, and he did; it didn't squirt out fifteen feet anymore. What the fountain did was to emit, grudgingly, a tiny trickle. The crayon scrapings were still there, but had been rearranged by Alex.

You turned the water on! said the very first youth in my first-period class. All entering students rushed to test it out; no one took anyone else's word for it. Shortly, of course, it was All Heart, Mr. Herndon! You turned it back on, but it don't work!

It does work, I say.

I have them there. It works. It don't work too good! they point out. I don't care. What *I* point out is that's *it* for all this going out into the halls to get a drink! *Fini, c'est tout!* I'm fond of saying.

By second period, here come Mark, Juliette, and Melinda, joined by Sarah, another Indian by way of Fiji, and Annie, a Samoan girl, smarter and *bigger* than everyone. Freed from work the last days, they are dying to confront me, on their ways to finding out the adult secrets of the universe. Finally! you can see them thinking. Annie and Sarah have been out of class the past two days for band practice. They have already been filled in about the water.

We go over it. You have to see that, going over it, we are all again as happy as larks. This is precisely what we are here for—they as youths, me as adult/teacher.

Now, I say, let's go back to the beginning. Somebody put crayons in the fountain, right?

Andy! they cry.

Fuck Andy! I say. I don't actually say that. Forget Andy is probably what I say.

I am in command now. They await my speech. How could I possibly say, Forget Andy? is what they want to know. Their whole upbringing, thus far, has told them about Andy and his fate, about Andy being identified and punished and they being scot-free to enjoy the fountain squirting all over the place.

While this is going on, Andy and his troops are getting the room cleaned out and put away, the end-of-school workers are working away, and there is continual demand for Sarah, Mark, Annie, et al. to be good guys and supply answers.

Now *when,* I say, when the fountain squirted out, what did you all think?

No one wants to talk about that. Bright, as all youths are, they can see the discussion is heading the wrong way. Youths are brave in their minds, but rarely when it comes down to it.

Annie is brave all the time, no doubt because she is a Samoan youth. We liked it! she says. You know we did! That's why you asked. She can see right through me, she implies. That was the most fun we ever had in this boring class!

The last will take care of me; it is all my fault, for having a boring class.

Everyone agrees loudly. *Exactly,* says Juliette seeing as how Annie said it and is still alive; if your class wasn't so *boring,* no one would have to put crayons in the water faucet!

Fountain, I say. Go on . . .

Mark says, Why do you insist on calling the water faucet a fountain? A fountain is something entirely different . . . and he goes on to describe fountains he has seen in this or that shopping mall.

I'm a little taken aback by this, because I don't know why I insist on it. So I give in and say that when I was a kid, that's what we called 'em. Building up courage, I'm about to say, after all, we didn't have these *plastic* shopping malls (*plastic* will get them!) . . . but then I am immediately met with a barrage of questions to the effect of How old are you? and various remarks about the Fall of Rome and the Civil War. You mean back when they were building the pyramids?

But they already know exactly how old I am, the result of such encounters earlier on, so I win. OK, I get to say, you all loved it when it squirted out fifteen feet. Point is, why did you all keep on squirting it out, after it was clear that it would squirt out fifteen feet?

They fall back. We didn't squirt it! Didn't do any of the above. It was true. They didn't have to.

You didn't have to, I remind them, but you liked it! I rush on. In a civilized world, people would see that the fountain squirted out fifteen feet and got everyone wet and their homework wet and caused a panic and was therefore no good. No good! Wait, stick around. Don't move . . . for they show every sign of having something important to do elsewhere. It's my turn.

And so, being civilized, no one would turn it on, or if someone did, you civilized people would tell them to stop it! Of course. No civilized person would *take pleasure* in that squirting out! Right? Of course!

So, I say, you are all barbarians! Being that the class is called social studies, it is a word I get to use and I am fond of it. Learning, reinforcement. *Barbarians! Fini,* I say, *c'est tout!*

Melinda interrupts this lecture by exclaiming over the grade book. Students check this book every day. They check it in order to see if I put down their own marks and also to see if I put down marks for anyone else who didn't deserve it. I am capable, they know, of anything. The book remains mysterious, with its little symbols and squiggles and runes, the meaning of which they can never be quite certain of, although I am happy to explain it every day, except that it is about life and death. That's why Juliette et al. are up here, trying to understand. Youth, however, is not going to understand me.

How can you be giving Andy a B minus? asks Melinda, outraged. She has caught me doing something not just unclear, but wrong.

I privately note that "how can you be giving" construction. The "I be, you be, he, she, it be" declension of black kids has caught on. It has become a standard. If Melinda uses it, everyone uses it.

They all crowd over the book to see, as they've seen before, that Andy has done no—not one—weekly assignment this quarter. So how can he be getting a B minus? It is hard to tell if they are triumphant or disappointed at having caught me out in some kind of . . . *unfairness,* is probably it.

What do you care what Andy gets? I ask sternly. You are all much too nosey anyway. I'm giving out the grades here.

In truth, they have nothing against Andy. Like everyone else, they like and admire Andy. They can't associate with him too much, because of his hard-line stance. Anyway, their concern is the fairness of the world, the primary youthful concern.

I point to Andy's grades on the tests. Two tests—one a pretty simple vocabulary test, the other a rather difficult map test. Andy got 100 percent on both. So he gets a B minus, I say.

But he didn't do any work at all! they cry.

Why are we here? I ask. To work, or to know something?

Both, says Annie, quite correctly. They are temporarily satisfied. They, after all, are getting A's both for working and for knowing something, plus this free gift of time at the end of the year. Mark has seen all this coming and is sabotaging the stapler, by turning the little platform around so that the staples come out backward. He does this almost every day.

Mark! I yell. Don't be sabotaging the stapler! I've also accepted "be" as a standard. Unlike "faucet" and "drink water," I like it, especially in conjunction with "don't."

I'm not quite finished with them. I know they suspect that Andy be cheating on the tests. I don't want them to have anything to hold on to. I call up Andy.

We go over to the big map, six feet by four or so, quite nicely drawn freehand and colorfully painted by some students in the first three or four weeks of school. It is there to study geography from, and displays the principal mountains and rivers and cities, etc., of Europe and the Middle East. None of them are labeled.

OK, Andy, I say, what's this river? I point to it.

Melinda and the rest watch carefully. They know it all.

Euphrates, says Andy, careful to betray no interest.
These mountains?
Carpathians.
This volcano?
Vesuvius.
This sea?
Adriatic. Can I go finish the books now?
Wait. This river?
Danube.

Thus endeth the lesson. The moral I've pointed out is, however, unacceptable. Andy is a ne'er-do-well, causes trouble, gets kicked out of class, sent to the vice-principal, does no classwork, and must therefore be *dumb.* That makes sense. But he isn't dumb. They go off, looking for a way out. They are youths and have no use for the real, just as we have taught them. I am little better off than they, and for the same reason. Of course, I'm grown up and accept the real, but I'm not supposed to around here. After all, in my role—hell, in my *job,* roles are not in my vision!—Andy is a pain in the ass. He is smart as hell and won't do anything. Thus he aggravates me, since it is somehow part of my job to get him to *do something,* indeed, do my assignments in the form of classwork. Well, "won't do anything" . . . he does plenty, all of it sneaky and disruptive. That shows considerable zeal, since it is not so easy to disrupt my class. I mean, you can disrupt some classes easily and innocently just by whispering, not paying attention, chewing gum, standing up, not opening your book, forgetting your pencil. We teachers aren't the same.

Note that all during this time, I (who have taught here more than twenty years and am quite secure in my job, as they say)—I keep in mind what is *officially* going on here, in case I have to tell someone who might ask. What is going on is a Final Review Lesson, Make-Up Work for those who have missed important assignments, Inventory and Storage of texts and other books by students (in itself a valuable lesson) while some students, A students the year long, alternately discuss issues with me or help these striving students whom you can see now, working away. I too am *in business,* and scot-free.

The question here is, whom are all these adults who worry about youth worried about?

Are they worried about Melinda and Mark and Juliette and Annie and Sarah and their perception of the real?

Are they worried about Andy and terrorism?

Are they worried about the panicking "extra-credit" workers, who are trying to get in a little overtime because the rent is due and report cards are coming out and they lost last week's paycheck drinking and playing liar's dice at the Lone Star Bar?

Frankly, it sounds to me as if these worriers are only people who went to school themselves a while back, ten or twelve or one hundred years ago, and have forgotten entirely what it was like, and so have made up a whole, new, imaginary school system to worry about.

From what I can get from the various media, now, in the summer of 1984, what they all are worried about is *me!* Me, and Harold and Peggy and Maggie and Gary and Clementine and Bob and Joe and Jane and the rest of us!

This national *worry* doesn't seem to be about Juliette et al., or Andy, or the late workers. (We, Harold and I and all, *we* worry about them.)

They don't seem to be worrying about Dave or Him or the school board. They worry some about the union.

These introductory pages are only here to remind you, readers, what a school is, and what it is for, and why it is there, and what goes on in it. It is only something to remember: there is nothing to learn.

The Pendulum

*What I then saw confounded and amazed me.
The sweep of the pendulum had increased in
extent by nearly a yard. As a natural consequence, its velocity was also much greater.*

—Poe

No one is going to admit that the crusade itself is no good.
Jefferson lives.

Right now, however, now that we are all official discontented citizens, discontented with our public schools, what do
we propose to do about them? How do we plan to correct
them? In what direction shall we proceed in order to raise
test scores, sell more cars, elect people running for public
office?

We need to look at the pendulum in order to see what we
ought to do. Please note, first, the time line.

The recommendations of Charles Eliot in 1893 have already

been mentioned, and the fact that, twenty-five years later, the pendulum swung back the other way.

By 1957 it was, on account of Sputnik, in full swing the other way. But by 1967, back it went again. It had taken only ten years to complete its cycle.

And now? It's 1985. The Committee on Excellence's report recommended more science, more math, more "time on task," more homework, and more discipline, firing teachers, more attention to technology (and *technology* was the same word used by Eliot in 1893). It was followed in *only six months* by the Carnegie report which said, No, no more math or science, instead more reading, more writing, no more homework, forget "time on task," think, make teachers' jobs more bearable, and the kids should do public service.

But if the pendulum is going to swing back now every six months, we are going to be in a situation more like poetry or revolution than ordinary citizens' discontent. We will be like Poe.

That awful *sweep!* That terrible *velocity!*

What, in God's name! shall we do? What are the ends, the poles, of this demonic swing?

Hold it, citizens! Before we collapse into terror and do something we wouldn't otherwise dream of doing, let's remember that we have been to school and therefore are not in the grasp of ignorance or superstition. We'll examine the pendulum, as Poe did, and get out of this.

At the poles of the pendulum are words, written as if on dungeon walls, luminous, perhaps, so that the captive may never overlook them. On one end the words will be, oh, achievement, the intellect, effort, authority, the future. On the other, socialization, democracy, the senses, freedom, the present. The captive sees the pendulum at one pole, hovering, and reads the luminous words and thinks, Right! Now it will stop! The pendulum has already begun its return swing.

The captive, mesmerized, awaits the momentary rest at the other end, then reads again and is, for a split second, sure that the ordeal is over.

In *Doctor Faustus,* Thomas Mann has the Devil describe Hell as consisting of two vast rooms, one hot enough to melt granite, and the other of a most intolerable cold, between which the inhabitants rush continually, for as soon as they are in the one, the other seems to be a heavenly bower. A wonderful description, one to excite the senses quite a bit and, if a bit harsher in consequence, quite in line with our pendulum. Back and forth; as soon as we are in one place, we must head, shrieking, for the other.

We have been to school and are not in the grip of superstition. We know that there is no Hell. That ought to tell us something about the pendulum.

Going back a bit, we know that neither pole is a heavenly bower. Even the Devil knows that. We have been to school and are not in the grip of ignorance either. Therefore, we know that there came an era known as Sputnik wherein it was clear that schools were not paying enough attention to math, discipline, homework, authority, and the future, and besides, the bloody Russians had this spacecraft up there. We blamed this on Progressive Education and freedom, and so on, and set about to remedy the situation. Ten years later, the luminous words told us that *that* hadn't worked, and all the students were dropping out and bored. Certainly, we had plenty of spacecraft. We invented "open" and "alternative" and "counterculture" and remedied that situation. Presently the razor-edged blade zooms past us, whispering, The schools are failing! Ah! We are confounded, and amazed.

We are now supposed to be in another Sputnik era. We'll remedy the thoughtlessness of the last Progressive era. But the very reason for the supposed Progressive era, like the reason for all such eras, is that the preceding Sputnik era didn't work, was itself no heavenly bower.

At the opposite ends of the swing are written, in small

print, the very same words. The pendulum swings from No Good to No Good, or from Not So Bad to Not So Bad, or from OK to OK. The same words appear at each end.

No matter which way the pendulum was said to swing, toward which pole, there was never any change. One reason is that no schools really ever changed in the slightest. *Whatever* it was, no one did it anyway.

That is exactly the same as saying that there is no pendulum at all.

4

Raffia

When I was in the fourth grade in Santa Barbara, our class went on a field trip. We went after lunch so that we could all eat lunch in the cafeteria, a lunch free not only to the poor, but to everyone. Maybe we were all poor in town, since this would have been 1935 or so.

Of course, we had been on field trips before. We had been to the roundhouse to see the trains switch and ridden in the cab of the locomotive. We had been to the Mission and to the natural history museum attached to it. We had been to the Courthouse. We had been to the Bird Sanctuary.

These were, however, *educational* field trips, from which we had to return to answer questions or write "essays" about what we had seen or heard. Even then, the school imagined that if we were not taken to these places, we would never know anything about them, although in fact we played daily on the grassy fields around the courthouse, wandered its tile-floored corridors and peeped into its offices; we hung around the trains, making plans to run away on these trains *someday*, (and saw men dropping off those trains who obviously *were* running away), we played around the Mission, we went down to the lake bird sanctuary and threw rocks at the birds . . .

We never went on a field trip to the WPA building where I, for one, accompanied my father every morning before going on to school. We drove down in his '29 Chevy, bought while he was still working and driven out here from Texas, and he went into his little office, and I hung around the courtyard to watch the men climb into the backs of pickup trucks carrying picks and shovels to go to work somewhere, and then I walked back and up the hill to school.

One place they went to work, I remember, was our own school, where they blacktopped an area which had been formerly just a dusty, weed-strewn lot, so that we could have a better place to play baseball and football. It seemed to take them a long time. Still, I don't really know if it did or not; the message was in the air, all that time, about how the WPA workers didn't exactly work all that hard. I went with my father every day to the WPA courtyard and watched the men and talked to them and wanted, one day when I grew up, to be allowed to climb into those pickups myself and go to work. I was quite capable, at the same time, of collaborating in the hoots and taunts directed at the same WPA men, at our school, and to believe that they were lazy and worthless.

Thus: the WPA men were different beings at the courtyard and at the school. A good lesson, had there been anyone around to give it. The blacktopped field may have been better for baseball and football, although certainly, when you fell down your elbow or knee got more severely scraped. At the same time, lizards and horned toads, which could formerly be found in that dusty field and taken into classrooms, were missing.

This field trip. Now it became clear to us (and God knows how many times the teacher had to tell us and explain it to us before it became clear!) that we were just going to go down to this little creek, near the beach. We were going to walk down there from school, spend the afternoon there, and then we could all just walk home. We all went to this creek all the time to try to catch crawdads and frogs and knew every inch of it. Still, innocents (not quite youths), we bragged to the rest of the school; while they were in school, we were just going down to the creek!

I still remember all about it. It was perhaps the highlight of my entire schooling. We did go. It was the same creek. We may have thought that the presence of the teacher and the school and us, *students,* of necessity, on a *field trip,* might have changed that creek into something that you could write an essay about. Perhaps the creek would suddenly have had Hoover Dam built across it! You could damn sure write an essay about that! (I recall we studied Hoover Dam quite a bit anyway.)

When we got there, the creek had not changed. It was the very same creek to which we went of our own free will.

That day, it gradually became clear to us that what we were to do at the creek was to gather willow branches. Well, there were plenty of them, and it looked as though we were being given a mandate to tear up the willow trees, rip off branches and leaves and throw them, fall into the creek, and have a hell of a time. Later on we were told the day was over and we left the creek and went home. We were tired by then anyway, played out and hungry.

The next day, however, we did the very same thing. We ate the school's lunch and trooped down to the creek. It is true that, beforehand, we had been informed that *since we were studying California Indians,* we were gathering these willows in order to make an Indian house—just as the Indians did, earlier on, and from the very same creek. I am not sure if I even knew, up until then, that we were studying Indians, although you may be sure that I was a model scholar. I guess it did not matter to me very much what it was we were studying. Anyway, as it turned out, we had not gathered enough of the *right kind* of willow branches, not really being Indians, and were going to get more.

When we got there, there was a man waiting, standing alongside a pickup truck. It was a '33 Ford, which was a pretty new car for us, and we admired it and got in it and crawled over it, until told it was time to go get the willows. Mrs. Smith (I'm almost sure that was her name—in any case I know I had a Mrs. Smith or a Miss Smith sometime around there) deferred to the man, let him order us around, tell us and point out what kind of branches to get—and, in the end, he got most of them himself, cutting them off neatly with a jackknife he pulled out of his pocket. Then we all piled all the suitable limbs in the back of his truck and he drove off.

It was a pretty satisfactory day too, and we were not surprised to see those willows, neatly trimmed of leaves and twigs, in our classroom the next morning. We were not surprised either, to hear that we were going to build an Indian house, right there in a corner of our room.

What we didn't know was that we were in the grip of a great revolution in American Public Education.

I know now that the progressive movement had us in thrall.

The professors at Columbia University had their eye on us and Ms. Smith knew it. She also knew that our parents might be a little surprised at us coming back from *school* all wet and dirty and happy from the creek, which was why she had lectured us firmly on what we were doing. She hoped, of course, that when we got home and were questioned, that we'd say, We're studying California Indians! But also, if we somehow didn't say that—and Ms. Smith, if a Progressive, showed us no sign at all of being crazy—she would have an ace in the hole to tell the principal when the parents called.

Learning by Doing! Ms. Smith would tell the principal, and all the principals and superintendents and school boards of America would have to stick by her, else John Dewey would have to have a word with them.

·   ·   ·

After our days at the creek, I would have given my full
support to the progressive movement, had I ever heard of it,
but that was about all the Learning by Doing we experienced
that year. We had the willows which, green and limber at
first, soon dried out and became hard to handle, and we had
heaps of raffia which, now that I look back, was one of the
main ingredients of the progressive movement, as if Columbia University had a corner on the raffia market. We were
supposed to just bend the branches and tie them together
with raffia, making a kind of dome, but it wasn't easy; nothing worked right and when it couldn't be done in fifteen
minutes we lost interest in it. If my teaching experience holds
true, we probably told Ms. Smith that this was *boring*, and
asked, How come we never learn nothing in here?

Ms. Smith persevered though, and the man showed up
again and got it built, probably helped by a smart, progressive kid like old Andy. We sat in the Indian house once in a
while, I recall, and no doubt it was the subject of some admi-
ration on Parents' Night.

Learning by Doing did not take over the rest of our curriculum nor our school hours, unless you count as Doing our
rote memorization and drill of multiplication tables, our writing of spelling words twenty times each, our answering of
questions about everything we read, our taking home and
Doing, or Not-Doing, homework. That was certainly not
what Columbia University had in mind by Doing. As for
Ms. Smith, I imagine that she was happy to have done her
part for the movement and to be able to forget about it for
the year. For, although my happy memory of those afternoons
at the creek is one thing, I know that Ms. Smith had to put
up with plenty of kids who spent the day crying because they
fell in the creek or because someone threw mud on them,
having to go to the bathroom, feeling sick, being too hot (or
too cold), having to call their mothers, and being too tired to
walk home.

In short, although the movement, a great national movement, was of vast importance, involving the praise or jeers of newspapers, radio pundits, politicians of every sort—you can find and read the annals of the progressive movement, the research, the clear and right declarations of need and *intent* to change—and although the movement was not tainted by involvement in voter registration or Vietnam protests or dope (as the school-movement in the sixties was), but instead was led by the most respectable people in the country—psychologists, scientists, philosophers—our school stolidly refused to change. A movement to *change education* in this country, it did not have anything to do with schools.

I'm sure there must have been official progressive schools, just as, later on, there were official alternative schools, but they were not *schools*. None of us common kids in the fourth grade had ever heard of one, nor heard of any kid who went to one. I believe my mother, who was certainly a progressive in many ways (my diet, for one thing, changing from goat's milk one year to orange juice with increasing drops of iodine in it the next, to orange juice with a raw egg in it the next), would have had the same attitude toward them as she did toward private schools, which was that they were places where people could send stupid rich kids who couldn't make it in the *schools*.

I do not mean to ridicule the progressive movement. Quite the contrary. When I took courses for my teaching credential one summer, they were all based on the tenets of Progressivism and I thought them quite sound, and still do, if you can leave out the belief in testing. But in our fourth grade, after the tasks listed above, we had lunch recess, where we saw that neither marbles nor real estate could be played on that blacktop, and, in the afternoons, a lady would come in to *give us music* . . . I remember, right now, the absolute thrill of hearing her sing harmony to "Home on the Range," the first time I ever got the idea of it. If she didn't come, Ms.

Smith *gave us* Art, and we had a band which you could go to if you agreed to "take up" an instrument. All these last items were quite amenable to Learning by Doing, perhaps because in order to learn them at all you had to be allowed to sing out loud, put on paint, and make noise on your horn.

We sometimes had P.E. with a teacher, before being turned loose to play dodgeball, which wasn't P.E. That is exactly what fourth graders do now. I bet thousands of fourth graders study California Indians (in California) right now; certainly the structure of their day is exactly the same as it was in 1935.

Actually, the only difference I can point to between my own fourth-grade school and elementary schools today is the free lunch. We were served Spanish Rice and Creamed Chipped Beef (also on rice), both of which I was very fond of and wished my mother would cook for dinner.

The lunch was free, as I've said, to everyone. We all just went in and got lunch and ate lunch. We have free lunch these days too, but only for those who will stand up and declare that they are too poor to afford to buy lunch. In order to do this, they must fill out forms *proving* they are too poor—there is a sliding scale, so much income, so many kids in the family. If you can't qualify for free lunch, you may indeed qualify for *reduced* lunch, admittedly an innovation. These free-lunch kids get their notices—you passed, you didn't pass—right in my classroom, brought in by a student messenger, where every kid snoops at every message which comes in. It is wonderful. You may imagine that there will be some friendly jesting back and forth between those kids who can pay and those who can't, and even that teachers may have to deal with this right after lunch.

We didn't even call it "free lunch," but only lunch. So the schools have actually gone downhill, in the progressive sense, since 1935. I doubt this lunch was the result of a demand by Columbia University; more likely an offshoot of some socialistic program in the Roosevelt administration. But lunch, hopefully Spanish Rice, served to all without charge, just as a matter of fact, will be my first demand in any movement to restore the schools to the enlightened place they occupied in 1935. Start there, comrades, and work up.

5

Plans

Happily, I'm supplied by a benevolent union with material describing all the plans in various states for improving the public schools, which are in disarray. Within this cornucopia, no pendulum, real or imaginary, is swinging. The plans, whether they have become law or are only suggestions, whether already funded by the state or not, whether from California or Tennessee, are remarkably the same.

We are going to have tougher educational standards! We are going to have excellence! That is that.

Specifically, students in high schools will now take at least three (sometimes four) years of English, at least three (sometimes four) years of math, at least three years of science, at least one year (sometimes more) of foreign language and, in most instances, one-half year of computer literacy, or, at Spanish Main, comp lit.

Variations occur only in details—that is, some plans spell

out one year of American literature, for example, in the three or four years of English. Some will require algebra for everyone among the three or four years of Math. Some insist on biology within the science program. Some say Spanish, specifically. The majority leave out such details, figuring that English is English, science is science, foreign language is foreign language, math, math, and that's good enough for them.

One such plan proposes to allow "tracking" in these required subjects; one refuses to allow tracking. All the rest leave that subject, once a major controversy, out.

Obviously, the requirements for graduation are to be increased to the extent just listed. (We are not going to have anyone graduating from high school claiming he or she can't read!) Moreover, competency tests must be passed, in most plans, at the end of junior high school, for a student to even get *into* high school. Graduating from the stage at Spanish Main may be in jeopardy.

Students must and *will* do Much More Homework, state these plans. No plan, if it hopes to be funded by any legislature, dares to leave out homework.

All plans demand more Time On Task—a popular catchphrase of the last three—four? five?—years, which apparently means spending more time on schoolwork in the classroom. Most plans see that more time on task can be achieved most easily by lengthening the school day and the school year. Well, that is logical. The time on task people place all their emphasis on the time part; what the task is (let alone, should be) is not part of the slogan. No doubt the *educational excellence* part of the plan, as above, is to take care of that.

The above is *what* the plans aim to do. All these plans then take up the *how* of it, to show that they are serious.

Opening up the *how* is Tougher Student Discipline. That seems to be basic to all plans. Every plan agrees that disruptive students will not, from henceforth, stop others from learning. They all use the same phrase—disruptive students. Some plans spell out this tougher discipline policy; others just say that they ain't putting up with it anymore.

Spelling out takes the form of listing penalties for the student who may wish to disrupt. These seem not to be novel, in the main. Suspension from class, suspension from school, expulsion—presumably for continued, willful disruption, and after conventional sentences like detention, notes home, and parent conferences have been handed out. The plans seem to be saying that, while they can't think of any *new* penalties—they don't suggest jail sentences, for example, nor allow teachers to shoot disruptive students—they mean these punishments, now, *to be carried out.*

So they say that students who continue to disrupt the pursuit of excellence won't be around for very long. The plans do not interest themselves in the future excellence of those students who, for cause, may not be around the school anymore. One or two do stipulate that if a student is suspended from a class for a period of time, that student may not be placed in another class during that time, recognizing, at least, something about a real, common practice of schools and putting a stop to it. A couple of plans suggest the possibility of "alternative programs" for disruptive students, one even using the phrase *school-within-a-school* (thus warming my heart).

All plans specify immediate suspension (and expulsion, if the deeds continue) for the traditional reasons—bad language, defiance of authority, insubordination, smoking, fighting, and now, the bringing to school of controlled substances. Only the California plan (the Hart Bill, SB 813) had a little footnote on the controlled substance part. While agreeing with the general tone of all other plans, this bill found it necessary to add "excepting for less than an ounce" of marijuana. It then amends itself with a little note about more potent kinds of cannabis, which do not fall into the less-than-an-ounce immunity.

Homework reappears here, in the how-to, discipline section of these plans. That is, teachers will be "authorized" to "give" homework to those students who may have been, for cause, suspended.

I believe that to be it about discipline. The plans, clearly, ain't playing around. I may add that the California Education Code, right around 1906, cited all of these indiscretions—fighting, smoking, defiance, etc.—as reason for suspension and expulsion. "Controlled substances" weren't mentioned, but the code did include, as reason for expulsion, "Filthy Habits!" which very possibly covered it.

I must add a little concern of my own about the California footnote. It sounds to me just like the injunction we placed, at Spanish Main School and many another—ten, twelve? thirteen? years back—against girls' skirts being too short, thus provocative, and interrupting the pursuit of excellence. That ukase caused many a principal and vice-principal and counselor and teacher to have to carry around a measuring stick in order to measure, in the flesh, if some girl's skirt was *in fact only* three inches above the knee, or whatever the dress code stipulated. It caused many a girl, also, to spend most of her time deciding whether or not to obey the command of the dress code, or to obey it sometimes and not others, or to disobey it flagrantly and then charge discrimination and quote some amendment, or to disobey it by a half-inch and get to spend most of her time in school gleefully being measured by all those hapless adults. I'm sure that activity did not fit in with the pursuit of academic excellence, and I fear that the California protocol, as it isn't yet called but certainly will be called, will not help us in that pursuit either.

We are still on how. How to do it—achieve excellence.

All plans call for "greater involvement" of community leaders and especially of "business" leaders. They call for the involvement of university, college, community college and city college professionals to improve the curriculum,

improve "methodology" and "teaching strategies," provide
leadership, show the teachers what to do. Alongside that, we
ought to remember that a primary suspicion, behind and
leading up to the plans, has been that these university, college, etc., professionals have always prepared students badly,
sometimes intentionally so, for the teaching profession. They
have been accused of being at fault to a great degree for the
incompetence of teachers everywhere. Perhaps the plans think
they have learned something in the meantime.

New, in the plans, is the heady agreement of "business
leaders." In California, there is something like a round table
of concerned businessmen, a big-time outfit it seems, which
agrees that the pursuit of excellence must be supported. Not
only that, but serious concern is demonstrated by the willing-
ness to put up *money* for this pursuit—money, in the form of
taxes! on businesses!

Money for what? For Sputnik? No, this time for "an educated work force." The business leaders claim that they are
tired of employees who cannot read or write, can't add and
subtract, and can't follow directions. Their expressed desire
is that their employees who show them a high school diploma
ought to be able to do these things, and they will spend
money to make it so. They subscribe to the *what* and the
how of the plans. (The present governor, certainly supported
for election by these businessmen, has not yet believed them
to be serious—granted, it's difficult to believe that business
really wants to have itself taxed—and so has not yet funded
any of the plans' measures which require money.*)

It is true that cynics (see chapter 3) may read beyond the
first paragraph of business reports in the paper and argue
that what is really needed in the work force is a group of
workers in service and fast-food industries, in the production
lines in Silicon Valley . . . people who will show up for

---

* In California, to everyone's surprise, the longer-day, longer-year money *did*
get funded, which just goes to show you. This money became the subject of
spirited bargaining, including many threats and a strike or two.

work on time to do a task (without going to the bathroom too often) which requires neither reading nor adding, nor a knowledge of biology, but only that kind of instruction which will enable them to be grateful for a job which is tedious, boring, and pays very little. Thus companies thrive. It may be that, at least in California, business executives ought to learn Spanish, for example; most of the work force imagined already knows it. The plans do not make comment, for that is not their purpose.

All the plans recognize that principals and other administrators must "learn, *and use*" better management skills. Here, we teachers agree. We don't know what these "skills" are, or should be, but we at Spanish Main are for it anyway. *Learn 'em and use 'em!* Right, we say. In Tierra Firma School District, we have a union/management committee going on right this moment, a committee which is trying to figure out a way for the district to "certify" that principals are "competent" to evaluate teachers. That's part of our reform bill (Hart) and must be done, otherwise the state will not fund the district. We can't begin to figure it out yet; the principals on the committee know, deep down, that they *are* competent (since they have been evaluating teachers for years) and the teachers on the committee believe that they are in no way competent, since they have been evaluating teachers for years.

The very reason for the above leads us to the rock-bottom impulse, and impact, of all the plans. Once principals are "certified" to be competent at evaluation (and this will certainly occur, no matter what the committee comes up with)— that will mean that they are able to spot those teachers who are incompetent, and begin the process of firing them. Not only that, but they will be able to point out those teachers who are truly great teachers, and thus begin the process of rewarding them.

All of the plans get down, finally, to the carrot and the

stick. They recognize that the classroom teacher is at the root of good and evil in the schools (as we do: "We're the team! We hit the ball, or no one does!") and figure to reward the one and uproot the other. Thus, all plans try to simplify lay-offs, simplify firing procedures, try to limit due process, try to limit tenure rules, for the bad guys. On the other hand, then all plans envision some sort of merit pay for the good guys.

The plans envision a kind of tracking system for teachers. Some will be judged to be in the high group (headed for Harvard), some in the average group (headed for city college), and some in the low group, headed for a production-line job at Silicon Valley, until the company decides to relocate in Korea, at which time the teacher relocates at McDonald's or Chuck-E-Cheez.

Of course, the idea is that the good ones, the teachers in the high group, will get paid more, and that will attract bright students to the classroom, because the pay will be good. That is the kind of thing businessmen understand. To prove it, the media tell us constantly that education majors in college are at the bottom of the class, intellectually. (The fact is that not one teacher in Tierra Firma School District was an education major in college.) However, once the evalu-ators are certified, then we can tell who is really good, and who is just OK, and who is worthless—something which earlier on had seemed very difficult—and get on with the pursuit rationally.

Last—well, it is only I who mention it last; it is first and foremost in every plan—everyone in the schools needs to put in more hours. Students do not put in enough *time* in schools. To that end, almost every plan proposes to put up some money for schools which agree to work more hours. In California, that plan envisions a payoff of between twenty dollars to forty dollars *for each student* if the school will increase its minutes per day to, say, three hundred, and/or if it will increase its instructional days to, say, two hundred. Most California elementary schools have instructional days of about 240 minutes in grades one to three; our instructional year is about 177 days.*

It is true that some analysts have calculated that if all the schools did increase their time on task to this extent, that the payoff in cash to the pursuit of excellence (and the public schools themselves) would about equal the national debt. It is thus no surprise that this incentive has not yet been funded by the governors.

The money, of course, would have to go to the teachers who would have to work longer hours and more days; it may be that, since no state can afford the price so far, that those teachers found to have merit, by the certified evaluators, will be those agreeing to work longer for the same pay. Longer hours, at no cost, is quite a decent business proposition, and can be called dedication, if need be.

It should be added that, in calling for longer school hours, the media and the politicians usually refer to such diverse societies as Japan, Soviet Russia, and Germany. We are urged to emulate their school hours, if nothing else. It is also true that in the same media, we can read or hear reports of Japanese educators complaining that their children have been only taught rote obedience, cannot think, and are committing suicide in great numbers—presumably because of their longer pursuit of excellence—and have come to America to get some tips about how to combat these ills.

So it goes. These are the plans, comrades. Do they mean anything? Hell, I don't know. I'm only trying to outline them here, but it is hard not to comment, however briefly. However cynically.

---

* In Tierra Firma, however, the upper grades and junior high students *already* go 308 minutes. Yet we maintain we still have problems. What can that mean? Well, three more *days* then, try that.

6

Of Time and Merit:
"What Are We Here For? To Work, or to Learn?"

Of course, as the plans wound through state legislatures on their ways to becoming law, various groups attached riders to them. The AFT, the NEA, school board associations, principals' organizations, PTA's—all had proposals meant to either strengthen or to weaken sections of the plans, and although all these proposals were made in the best interest of the schools, they often coincided with the best interest of the proposing group. The legislators had to try to please everyone and so inevitably the plans resemble the elephant being examined by blind men; from one place they resemble snakes, while from another nothing so much as a tree trunk.

Many of the proposals are really just cold compresses to the headaches and exasperations of someone—someone *discontented,* in a particular way. Homework is a nice solution, for example, for the worried parent who feels that if the kid was home doing his homework, he wouldn't be out smoking dope. The idea, however, does nothing for the teacher who has already been *giving* the homework, but sees that the kid isn't *doing* it because he is allowed by the parent to go out and smoke dope.

Just so, it is wonderful for the teacher to hear that students may no longer disrupt the classroom, since teachers, through their organizations, have protested that if they did not have to spend all this *time* with disrupters, they could really teach and the other students really learn. The plans have heard the teachers and responded. The plans, although they do not say so, don't really mean to deal with *violent* students—those stories in the paper of the girl shooting up a school with her brother's .22, or rival gangs shooting it out from cars in front of the high school; these incidents are not "disruption," any more than a bomb is disruption. *Disruption* is the girl who gets up and sharpens her pencil just as I'm ready to begin part 3 of my marvelous retelling of the Trojan War, or at least it is if she does this *every time* just when I've gotten the class settled down and ready to attend, the students dying to learn, me dying to teach . . . Disruption is when I say nicely, Please wait to sharpen your pencil, and she says I have to sharpen it, how can I take notes otherwise? and *I* say, Well, you should have sharpened it beforehand! and she says, How could I? So-and-so took it from me and I had to take it back! How could I sharpen it if he . . . and *he* says, That's a lie! I never saw . . . ! The patiently and surreptitiously unscrewed desktop falling to the floor with a crash, the fountain squirting out fifteen feet, the resulting glee and uproar of the class, free of retribution and blame, *free* for the moment— so that while the legislature has heard the teachers and given them their due, they have probably not reached old Andy, who probably knows about as much about these reforms as I, in the fourth grade, did about the progressive movement.

None of this does anything really for the teacher, who will continue to deal with it patiently, understanding the student, firmly, understanding the needs of the class, and finally with exasperation, saying in the teachers' room, This kid is driving me nuts! It does little for the parent either, who phones up the school and wants to know how come the kid is kicked out of class for sharpening her pencil?

Most plans heard the teachers too, on the subject of "adjunct duties," as they are called in California. Those are duties, say teachers, which take them away from teaching school—bus duty before and after school, cafeteria duty, playground duty, hall duty, detention duty. The California plan, at least, responded by removing adjunct duties from the evaluation sheet, which meant that principals would no longer evaluate teachers on the basis of excellence at these duties. That was, of course, the only objective item in the whole list—either the teacher was on time for duty or not, either made it to bus duty or not, or had a good excuse.

The other items were always something like "maintains suitable learning environment," which could mean (and does mean) variously, that the teacher has pretty, decorated walls, or that the windows are open exactly right, or that the room is quiet, or that it is suitably animated, or that kids don't sharpen pencils while the teacher speaks . . . and then, something about learning, like "students demonstrate a year's growth, or are working up to their abilities." Added to that, usually something about "adherence to the district curriculum"—meaning you were teaching California Indians, not the Crimean War. There was enough in there for the principal to be boss with, and enough totally subjective and unmeasurable for the teachers' security. After the sixties, references to personal attributes disappeared from the evaluation sheet in most places, certainly in Tierra Firma, where outraged teachers no longer read that their dress is inappropriate, that they are bad for morale, that they have halitosis.

Still, taking away adjunct duties from the boss left a hole, apparently, and the relatively harmless clause was replaced by an ominous "appropriate teaching strategies" in many plans. But since that seemed to imply that some strategies were better than others (and for *strategies,* we teachers read *styles!*) and it certainly seemed as if principals were to decide this matter of style, then these administrators better be certified as competent to do so and the committee in the district to make recommendations concerning this better have some teachers on it to protect their interests.

After all, we at Spanish Main remember Him calling a faculty meeting for the purpose of informing us that He had been in all our classrooms, and not a one of us could be observed passing back the kids' papers correctly. We can see this, or something like it, getting in there with these strategies, and, to head it off, we teachers on the committee argue that teaching is an art, and as such, different teachers have different styles, all of which may be excellent, if different, and that principals must agree to this if they are to be "competent" to judge us. The issue is not settled yet. In the end, the school board will have to make a Policy on strategies; the plans have listened to the school board's association too and given these boards final authority over all this. By and large, school boards are not capable of making such a policy, so that in the end some statement containing the word *individual* will likely emerge, which will satisfy everyone, except whoever wanted *strategies* in there in the first place.

(What method should we use for passing out papers, did you ask? Well, in the interest of efficiency and time on task, we ought to face the class, where the students are sitting in rows. We ought to have arranged the papers beforehand in order, so that when we give the stack to the first student in a row, that student simply takes the top one and passes the stack back to the second student, who also takes the top one, and so on, down the rows. We will have wasted no time in a *noninstructional activity;* there has been no reason for disorder or disruption.)

It is clear that the plans really had two major objectives in mind, objectives which, to be sure, have been there in the minds' eyes of politicians, educators, media, and public for some time, and whose time has come. These notions are the longer school day, and some form of merit pay for teachers, and these have been approached much more confidently and definitely.

Early one morning in the Dallas airport, I read in the paper that Texas educators were calling for students to spend an "eight-hour day" at school. This was to be all students, grades one through twelve. More time in school; a longer school day, and more days, has been a feature of every plan. I could never see why, unless, given what everyone thinks of as the "failure" of the progressive movement, the failure of Sputnik and the New Math, the failure of open classrooms and counterculture, and the failure of back-to-basics/phonics, a lot of people have just said to themselves (whether at Columbia University or the Department of Education or at the editor's desk in Dallas) that, goddammit! the longer you do something, the better you'll get at it, and we'll just keep 'em in there longer. Anyway, we've already tried ever' other goddamn thing . . .

Of course. There has, after all, never been any research to corroborate such an idea. Indeed, there has been plenty to suggest the opposite . . . all the way from major experimental studies which showed that twelve-year-olds who never went to school at all "progressed" a year on standardized tests simply because they had grown a year older, a fact not dependent upon plans, to someone like Max Weber commenting that his only true ideas came when he was doing nothing, or perhaps shaving, never when he was "studying." Sure, a comrade of mine, in our old school-within-a-school, wrote upon her chalkboard, every day, "One learns that which one practices," for the edification of her students. What she meant, though, was that the students should "practice" (in this case, *read*) intently for some fifteen or twenty minutes a day. That would be plenty, she thought. (Indeed, our whole school, Rabbit Mountain, was finally predicated on this notion, that the students should do intensively, and for a short time, one thing—in this case, learn to read. Did it work? We thought it did; I leave out here any description of disruptions during the rest of the day.)

Anyway, thanks to the Dallas airport and the morning paper, I'm no longer confused about the issue. After all, the studies to the contrary were part of some progressive movement; Max Weber was a genius; Rabbit Mountain was a radical, alternative school, however "within" a real school. None of those things counts, as we know.

Dallas gave it away. The point is, the paper said, quoting the Texas educators, that students will "work an eight-hour-day, just like the regular work force."

Now we get it, I think.

I thought it nice, though, as the article went on and I, having nothing else to do, read it all, that the main objections to this eight-hour plan came from the football coaches. Football is a major occupation, or preoccupation, in Texas, and the coaches could see that this eight-hour day was going to cut into practice. You can get the notion, from some Texas coaches, that attending class, for some good football players, is just a pain in the ass, something of no value, but which you just have to put up with.

The Texas educators were talking about an eight-to-five job of being students. At the end of the article, however, I noticed that they had paid attention to the coaches (and perhaps to the fact that they lived in Texas) and had proposed that, although students must stay in school until five o'clock, the hours from 3:00 until 5:00 could be spent in "extracurricular" activities, supposing that the student had a certain bent or interest in same. I got it; that meant art, music, theater, clubs of any sort, or—football practice.

"Just like the regular work force." So it is not complicated at all. By recommending an eight-to-five day, the Texas educators, and the plans of every other state in this union, the businessmen, the politicians (note there's nothing at all in

these plans about education, no time to wonder about learning) just means that an *educated work force* is one which will
spend eight hours on the job, and not go to sharpen a pencil
when they spozed to be putting out the product.

That ought to be it. Still, I can't help it! I have this clipping from some magazine or other, I no longer know, which
says (written by some guy named Rutter, the clipping says)
that homework is but of "symbolic importance"; it empha-
sizes the school's "expectation that students have the ability
and self-discipline needed to *work* without direct super-
vision." Students, in short, ain't to learn anything from
homework, except symbolically to *work*.

*The idea that if you're paid more you'll work
harder may apply to selling encyclopedias. If
you're a lion-tamer, you're not going to work
any harder just because you'll be paid more.
The job of a teacher is more like a lion-tamer,
I think.*

—AL SHANKER, President
   AFT, AFL-CIO

I've tried hard to find something to say, pro or con, about
merit pay—something that has not already been said hundreds of times. Shanker's remark, above, is one point of view.
You must work hard, as a schoolteacher, simply in order to
avoid being eaten alive. Subduing the lion's natural appetite
comes first—after that is assured, maybe you'll be able to
teach him a trick or two.

Merit pay has been around a long time in the corporate/
industrial world, but even there no one seems satisfied with
it. No research can be found which agrees that the salesman
works harder or is more *successful* at his trade if he is given
extra pay for "merit."

It is, anyway, quite beside the point whether one works
hard or not. Success is the point. But even there, sales man-

agers report that no one is satisfied if the person who *demonstrably* sells the most of whatever product it is, is paid more. The other salesmen argue that they had bad territories, mix-ups in their deliveries, no cooperation from the front office, storms—otherwise they would have been right up there.

Teachers, like salesmen, all believe that they are among the very best at their job. You simply must believe that in order to continue teaching (and probably selling).

You begin to teach as a lion-tamer, to be sure and, if not eaten up, go on to ask other teachers what they do here and there, what "works" for them, and quite soon, by some curious amalgam, you develop a way to work in the classroom which suits you and which you think is best . . . best, considering the various and vast distances between what you must do, want to do, and can do.

You think it best, for you and the students, or for the students and you.

I certainly think that my "style" or "strategy" in the classroom is the best. That's why I do it that way. I also know that my opinion is not shared by the other teachers at Spanish Main, each of whom, quite rightly, prefers his own.

The whole idea of merit pay, then, seems to founder at this point. If we all think that we are among the best, how are we to reward the best?

If we must decide who is the best, then who is to decide, and on what basis?

The plans suggest a committee, even that this committee (in most cases) be composed of a majority of teachers, so that teachers can see that their professional judgment is valued. Yet, if the above is true, it doesn't seem likely that teachers can make such a decision, nor has any basis for a decision been provided.

The famous Tennessee plan decided to solve the problem by having independent teams of evaluators roam around Tennessee judging on the merit of teachers. This notion did away with the sordid suspicions of local favoritism, school board politics, and ass-kissing, to be sure, but doesn't appear to help with the main problem. For this traveling team will either have to announce its visits in advance, or not. If they do, the scene will be like an army inspection, or Mayor Daley erecting fences to hide the slums of Chicago at convention time. The teacher, if not crazy, will redo bulletin boards, get every kid's goddamn pencil sharpened in advance, send Andy to the library, or *somewhere,* figure out a wonderful demonstration lesson (well practiced in advance by all), and all will go well.

But if the team drops in as a surprise, they may come into my seventh-grade reading period to find me either standing, elbows resting on my bookcase, or sitting behind my desk, reading from *Captains Courageous,* or from *Sports Illustrated.* I may be oblivious to their entrance, in fact. (I am not oblivious to kids talking, copying homework, wandering around—my ear is fine-tuned to these sounds, the sounds of activities which are forbidden since they aren't *reading*—but how is the visiting team to know that?)

The visiting team, concluding that this teacher is not teaching *at all,* let alone well, is not dedicated, doesn't give a damn, certainly deserves no merit pay (if he deserves to be paid at all!)—the team has just missed out on one of the best teachers in the world! They are unaware of it.

Too late, then, for my thoughtful discourse on what teaching is, how students learn, etc.!

Has something been left out in this discussion? I want to cover everything about this now; I never want to return to it.

Well, the basis is left out. The standard, criterion, measure, rule of thumb . . . *anything,* any way by which to tell the great teachers from the simply OK teachers. The standard, etc., by which to tell the wonderful teaching strategies from the mediocre ones.

Are the great teachers more entertaining? Have they better intellectual command of their subjects? Have they greater rapport with the students? Are they more efficient, provide more time on task? Are they more aware of their students' ethnic backgrounds, social class, personal or family problems? All of the above? Well, *some* of the above?

No one knows.

Does anyone know whether students actually *learn more* from great teachers, if you could ever find out who were the great teachers?

No one knows that either. The sentence just above sounds insane.

In the city where I live, right next to Tierra Firma, the school administration has often released to the newspaper the bad news that *on a normal day,* about 50 percent of high school students are actually in school. Only if attendance drops significantly *below* 50 percent do they wonder if something unusual is going on. One main problem with high schools, then, is that half of the students don't go to them regularly. If we believe the current reformers, this leads to low test scores and an uneducated work force.

Is the answer to this problem more time in school, more days in school, more homework? Will another hour each day bring these discontented students back to the high school from the beach, the movies, their jobs, the street corners? I think it more likely that there is another ten or fifteen percent of the school population who are now just barely hanging in there each day, just making it to the last bell by the skin of their teeth, barely managing to control their exasperation, frustration, and boredom, as it is. Another hour in such a day, another hour's homework, one more English, math, science course may just drive them over the edge into real discontent, to where the beach or McDonald's looks pretty good to them. Well, those left will compose an educated work force.

Has it been shown that the great teachers (if we knew who they were!) in the high schools have a higher percentage of students attending regularly?

One could, of course, consider paying all teachers more money, although that would not require any plan. Failing that, I'd agree to pay some teachers more money on merit, if we could just decide the issue by lottery, or matching pennies, two out of three, and change every year.

At least we will have dealt with merit. No living human being can make any sense out of time.

7

A School Kit

Model airplane kits, when I was young, could be bought for a dime, and contained plans and balsa wood parts. Glue was not included.

Finished, the model looked like an airplane, or, at least, more like an airplane than it did anything else. You would not have confused it with a model car, for instance, or with a school.

It looked like a plane and it was fun to put together and even to admire. It was not an airplane though, and we never thought that it was. We knew you could not get in it and fly to New York.

There has been some mention of *strategies* in the classroom, with the clear implication that some are better than others. (We now know that every teacher still alive believes that too, and knows that those better strategies are his own.)

Nevertheless, earlier on a strategy about passing out papers was mentioned. This strategy pointed out that if we would just pass out papers this way, we teachers wouldn't lose time from our instructional purpose. It was also pointed out that we weren't, *not a one of us,* doing it this way. This strategy didn't belong to any one of us.

It may seem to be a small thing, but the question is, Why *aren't* we all doing it?

Can't you even get with it enough to pass out papers right? I hear the plans asking.

Take a look at this strategy. First of all, we arrange the papers according to rows, first to last. That takes a little time, but maybe we can have our student aide, Pamela, do that . . . anyway, assume we do that.

But wait . . . some of us find that students move their seats every once in a while. Kids sit happily in some place for a while, and then find they would rather sit somewhere else. They do that for various reasons—they changed friends, so-and-so is getting them in trouble, so-and-so is not trouble enough. Some teachers let the kids move, depending on the outcome of the move; others have a firm seating chart, and no one moves. If you got your papers all in order, by rows, but then that morning you find that some kid has *moved,* that's it for the strategy. No one knows when a kid will decide to move. So therefore, *no kid moves.* OK, let's go on.

Next, you stand in front of the class and give out the papers by rows. The first kid takes the top one, the next kid ditto . . . and so on. In three minutes it's all over, *fini, c'est tout;* on with instruction.

But wait! What if one of the kids in the row takes the bottom one, by mistake? Kid wasn't listening when you ordered the strategy. What if some kid, not by mistake, decides to look through the papers and, say, yell, So-and-so got an F! Hey, you got an F, you dummy; or some other more pejorative word. Or, as it may be, So-and-so *cheated,* that's why he got an A, Mr. Herndon! This ain't my paper! cries the first kid. You bitch! yells the second. Did I cheat? the third appeals to someone next to him. You copied me! yells a fourth, fifth, . . .

This clearly is not working. In order for it to *be* working the teacher will have had to spend a week discussing, clarifying the procedure, the strategy, even if the students have seen this same procedure for seven years. In order for it to work, the teacher will have to shout, command, order, threaten—all with great and intense vigor—in order to make the class sit still, shut up, pick up the right paper, not comment upon the work of others, and get these papers passed out, so that we can get on with *learning*.

This strategy, then, is fine for a school kit.

Now how it works in a *school* . . . well, I don't know, I never thought about it much. I guess I just wait until some day when the papers are ready to hand back, until some such time as the students are individually engaged in some class-work—or supposed to be engaged in it—and I'm going around helping them or encouraging them or insisting upon it and there is always a student or two dying to pass out papers and I give them the papers and they pass them out. While it is true that many of the same comments and accusations may arise, and that there may be arguments about who gets to pass out the papers, it does not seem to be quite the same as the above. It has not been a big deal, but just, rather, a part of the day, easily handled, and the papers are, sooner or later, passed out.

That is the difference between a school kit and a school. In the school kit, nothing may be allowed to disturb the strategy, for that is what the strategy is there for, to be undisturbed. In a school, attended by the common people, and taught by the common people, the controversies attendant upon the passing out of papers are part of the instructional day, as interesting and valuable, I think, as much else; above all else, unavoidable, unless you have decided to spend all your time, and all your students' time, in this school kit, practicing and learning how to pass out papers.

8

Chanh

"The Helping Hand Strikes Again."
—JOHN HOLT

When Chanh came into my social studies class, some years back, sometime in November I think, I didn't quite know what to do with him. The problem was that it was social studies, and the silly social studies book, which I was always being ordered to use, and that Chanh spoke and read no English. He may have been the first Asian of this *particular* sort that I came across in class. That just means he wasn't City Chinese or Tokyo Japanese whose father, a banker, was transferred out here to the West Coast for a bit. Refugee, escapee, emigré, tourist? I never quite knew.

Since I didn't know what to do with him, I didn't do anything at all. I mean, I came by his seat two or three times each period and said, How you doing? and he grinned and I could see that he was looking at his Non-English-Speaking

(NES) dictionary or book or perhaps just pretending to—
well, my recommendation to teachers has always been, in case
of doubt, do nothing. I don't mean that this advice is often
taken, and certainly was never asked for. It is hard for teachers to do nothing, just as it is for kids to do nothing. Both
seem, when faced with a situation where they don't know
how to proceed, to fuck up. They do so with different inten-
tions, of course.

After a time Chanh discovered that unlined, white ditto
paper was available for use in the class, that he could go get
it, take it back to his desk, and draw on it. He discovered it
by scientific method—saw it in a neat pile near my desk, saw
other students go get it, saw them draw on it, tried it himself, awaited some severe blow—receiving none, he was in
business.

He left the NES book and NES dictionary alone then and
drew on the white paper. Now when I passed by his desk he
was always drawing, mostly animals—drawing with a nice,
fine, tracery line which I admired. He looked up at me tenta-
tively as I passed, to see, I thought, if it was OK. He sharpened his pencil a lot, perhaps happy to see that the pencil
sharpener was also readily available.

It ought to be mentioned that old Chanh, I knew, was en-
rolled in two English as a second language classes in our
school (ESL, we say) on his way to graduating from being
NES to LES (Limited-English-Speaking) and thence, if all
went well, to be *mainstreamed.*

As it happens, I was living down on Clement Street at the
time, and therefore dropped in often after work at the Lone
Star Bar. The Lone Star was run by a guy from Arkansas, a
retired army sergeant of artillery, and its clientele came
mostly from the Presidio, the old San Francisco army base,
thus enlisted men from Arkansas, Texas, Georgia, Alabama,
and such. The guy's name was Jones, called Jonesy, and he
knew I was a teacher. One day he asked me if I had any kid

who could draw good. What he needed, he said, was somebody who could draw a good, big picture of this razorback
hog, which he had a good picture of to copy, and the reason
he needed it was that the Arkansas-Texas football game was
coming up on the TV that Thanksgiving, everyone would be
there at the Lone Star Bar, and he needed it to jive the damn
Texans with. I could see that, and allowed as how I could
handle it.

So I gave the Lone Star picture of the razorback to Chanh,
provided a great big piece of good, white drawing paper, and
Chanh started off. He drew it in pencil first, stopping over
and over again to use the pencil sharpener. Later I produced
red and black markers, the big, thick kind, and we'd say
words to each other like *color,* and point out to each other
where red, *where* black. In any case, we fooled with it every
day for a while, and we could see it was going to be nice.

Now the picture I'd got from the Lone Star had a slogan
over it, saying, "Go Razorbacks!" One day Chanh looked up
from his drawing and asked me, "What is Way-Zo-Bak?"

We went round and round about razorbacks, and as the
drawing was done I felt Chanh had something of a notion of
what it was all about—football, the hated Texas Longhorns
(what is "Longhorn"?), the TV, Thanksgiving Day. In fact, I
began to feel that, for people doing nothing, we had made
considerable headway. I took the razorback drawing over to
the Lone Star, after promising Chanh to give it back to him
afterward. It was truly a good picture—a mean, snorting,
bristly hog with bad-looking tusks, done in heavy reds and
blacks so that you could see it from the bar. Jonesy thought
it was wonderful and bought me a drink, in itself something
unusual.

Well, a good lesson for all, I thought. I had started Chanh
off, and also Jonesy. By and by, they'd get together.

But the Monday after the Thanksgiving holiday, in came
Chanh. He was crying. It was third period. He came up to

me at the beginning of third period with tears rolling down his face.

I figured that some kids had been tormenting him, and got mad. "What's the matter with Chanh?" I demanded of everyone, really angry. No one knew. They were all innocent. Finally some kid said, "I had him last period, and he wasn't crying then." *He* hadn't done nothing, the kid meant.

"What's wrong, Chanh?" I said. I figured someone had done something to him during passing period. Chanh was a little tiny kid, very skinny, and he looked like another Chanh whom I had in class just this last year and whom the black kids called E.T.

"Way-Zo-Bak *lose!*" he cried, snuffling and wiping his eyes with his sleeve. "Mr. Herndon, Way-Zo-Bak lose!" He fairly hollered out the last, full of anguish.

Holy Christ! I'd watched the game myself and it was true that Arkansas lost, and very likely old Jonesy had lost some money, as well as having taken a lot of shit from the damn Texans; but *Chanh?* We began to talk, in our odd way, and I got it that his whole family, his father and mother, his grandmother, his sisters, some cousins, had all watched the game, and that when those Way-Zo-Bak lost, they had all gone into mourning. As if Chanh's picture had been a kind of talisman and, not having worked, it was a bad sign for all. No, he did not want the picture back.

I put my arm around him and consoled him and all, and told him it wasn't so bad, and tried to get it over to him about *next year*. I thought he got that, and told him that his picture would stay there until next year at the Lone Star (God knows what he thought the Lone Star was!) and then, next year, maybe, Way-Zo-Bak *win!*

So perhaps it was OK. Doubtless I could have informed Chanh that he ought to try an *s*, as in "Way-Zo-Bak*s*." Well, I didn't, and I know that Chanh spent the next weeks until Christmas vacation with his NES book and his NES dictionary. Occasionally he would bring up one or the other and ask me something. He didn't come back to school after Christmas vacation and, as usual, the school didn't say why, or where he had gone.

At that time there were a lot of people like Chanh going to Minnesota, so perhaps he went there. I'd hope not, since *Minnesota lose!* Maybe his old man was a banker, or a real estate agent, and he got to go to L.A.

9

Pamela Brown

Last year, the girl who was sharpening her pencil just when I was going to begin part 3 of my installments of the Trojan War was very likely to be Pamela Brown. We've already been through what I said, and she said, and the rest of the class then got to say.

This year, old Pamela is in the eighth grade, and eighth graders, at Spanish Main school, get to be classroom aides, supposing they can get some teacher to agree to it. Often the reason they want to be aides is that they don't care for the other offering of the school, as far as electives are concerned. The eighth graders get to choose two, from among art, foreign language (Spanish, French), music, shop, home ec, media, journalism, and yearbook. There are also library aides, health office aides, and main office aides. We don't have any strategies for all this; we just offer it.

Pamela had apparently chosen some of the above, but by the third week of school could see that one of them wasn't going to work out. She asked me, could she be my aide? Sure, I said, although uncertain about what I would have her do. In the end, another comrade and I shared Pamela, first period, finding flunky work for her to do, and it has been OK. Officially, my comrade has Pamela put grades in the book, do this and that; I have her pass out papers.

I've also another plan for her; she is to take on three students in my first-period class, all certifiably bright, but who are no good (don't do the work, don't pay attention, and so on) and get them in line. They are all good friends of hers, as I know. I tell her if they flunk, she flunks. She argues against this plan. She knows that aides are supposed to get A's just for doing this flunky work. You're the teacher, she tells me, not me!

For the first two quarters of this year, the three got two C minuses and one D. Pamela got an A. You would think that would convince her that the whole plan, the strategy, was bullshit. But it didn't. She is still exhorting the three (when done with passing out my papers, done with flunky work for my comrade) to *get to work, otherwise Mr. Herndon will be giving me a bad grade!* She is angry at them, at the same time as she is running about the classroom, exchanging gossip, egging cats on, being, as she was before, disruptive. I would not get no merit pay, just on account of Pamela.

It is true that now, the three are doing better. Bernard, for one, is heading for an A. Yolanda, all set for a B. Well, the third, not doing a hell of a lot better. A C, maybe. Better than a D. Whose strategy is responsible for this improvement, mine or Pamela's?

Never mind. Let me report about just this last Thursday. I've "given" part 3 of the Trojan War, to the class, on Wednesday. This chapter is about the bloody Greeks, after eight years in Troy, raiding those little islands around there. Well, one night, at this island—What island? asks some pedant; I don't know, I say, pointing to the map, there's a million little islands there, never mind that *anyway,* and I go

on to describe the problem with Cryseis and Bryseis, Agamemnon and Achilles, where Achilles, full of wrath, says he
isn't going to fight for Agamemnon or the Greeks.

Privately, I plan to deal with the pedant later. I do know
the island, but that ain't the point.

You all better write this story today, I say, since you'll forget by tomorrow. Also, I'm erasing the names off the board
at the end of the period.

I've told my story, about fifteen minutes' worth, and I
want them to "summarize" it—write down the story—now.
I've no other plan for the day. Thus the threat. These are
hard names; Cryseis, Bryseis, Achilles, Agamemnon, Ulysses.

That's Wednesday. Pamela's kids, Bernard and all, naturally don't do it. Their deadline, as I've told them, is Thursday. The deadline for the other students is Friday. How
come, etc., has already been dealt with, and Pamela is in
agreement. Because you'll wait till Friday, she says, and then
you won't get started till the last ten minutes, and then you'll
forget it and then you just won't do it, and I'll get an F. That
is what Pamela always did, and she knows that she is right.
So do they.

On Thursday, I start working around the room, helping
here, exhorting there, as usual on Thursday. It's their day to
work, get the assignments done, ready for Friday. Over in the
corner, I see Pamela holding court with her students and
some others. Hell, I think, and go over to straighten this out,
get everyone seated, working, and so on. They are all standing up, arguing loudly, and the place is a mess.

Full of wrath myself, I plan to throw out a couple, and
lecture the rest. To my surprise, Pamela seems to welcome
my advance. Mr. Herndon! she cries.

Ain't it true that the ol' King Agamemnon stole Achilles'
girlfriend, and now he ain't going to fight and the Greeks
can't win without him? And that's why the whole thing happened later, because he took his woman, because he's the
king?

All in one breath. Pamela is mad. These seventh graders are arguing with her.

And Achilles said he was going to kill him, but Ulysses said calm down, only a woman, just give it up man, so Achilles said, OK, but I ain't fighting for him, or you!

Pamela didn't hear the story yesterday, Wednesday, since she was working for my comrade, down the hall. She heard it last year in my language class.

Pamela Brown remembers it. Pamela Brown can say Achilles, she can say Cryseis and Bryseis, she can say Ulysses.

Pamela Brown can say Agamemnon with ease. Can Captains of Industry do that? Can Reagan do that? Can Bill Honig do it?

I myself was as happy as any lark.

PART II

Some Good Schools

You ought to teach a child a random combination of fantasy, simple
truth and outright lies. The Giant's
Garden, cows eat grass, and pigs can
fly. That will serve to keep the
child's mind alert, down to earth,
and wary.

JACK SPICER

— 10

Summertime

No sense of proportion. And it was a sense of proportion, above all things, that Brookfield ought to teach—not so much Latin or Greek or Chemistry or Mechanics. And you couldn't expect to test that sense of proportion by setting papers and granting certificates.

—MR. CHIPS

It seems to be my fate to run across obsessed dogs. In *How to Survive,* I wrote about the old, obsessed Bolinas dog, with its tennis ball. I realize now that I also mentioned dogs running into classrooms—perhaps they had to be obsessed too, in order to do such a thing.

In the summertime, as I began to write much of the foregoing, Arpine and I were house-sitting for friends who were taking a trip to Europe. The place itself was just far enough from the bay to be hot in the summer, it had a nice garden to fool with, and plenty of stuff to water, so that much time could be spent in that kind of work which gives one a feeling of having worked and having done right, without having to *know* anything—the perfect atmosphere for writing. There was a swimming pool, and it was usually some ninety degrees outside.

There was also a middle-aged German Shepherd bitch whose name was Anna K. but whom I, for some reason, immediately renamed Billie Jean. We had been warned not to try to pet Billie Jean, or to let her out of the backyard; had been advised that she would, and should, sleep at the foot of our bed, and that she did not like men. These rules were not for our protection, since Billie was not vicious and wouldn't bite; they were for hers.

Fair enough. The injunction against men proved true. After a week or two Arpine could pet Billie; when *I* reached out my hand she fled. Jack and Jay, my sons, came by to stay a bit; neither could succeed in petting Billie. *Not even Jay?* Jesus! Jay has been known to have squirrels crawl into his lap, wild ducks alight on his head, rattlesnakes lick his toes . . . Billie Jean fled.

Now, when I (or any of us, but I'll stick to me) go into the pool, Billie's obsession gets into action. I sit outside in the patio, read the paper, write a few words, and decide it's time for a swim. I plunge in. Billie Jean hightails it in a number of directions, one of which produces an old, beat-up ball, about the size of a softball but with no insides, so that it is crushable and may be easily snapped up by Billie Jean.

OK. She gets it, and, as I swim or dive or float, Billie rushes around the pool lickety-split, the ball in her mouth, pursuing me wherever I go, wherever I end up after a lap, a dive . . . there is Billie Jean, ball in her mouth.

Billie Jean is a big dog, she is confined to this backyard mostly, and *I know* that she wants me to throw the ball for her to chase. When I surface at one end or side of the pool or another, she is right there. The rules say that she is supposed to drop the ball, or let me take it from her jaws. Then I will throw it, she will happily chase it, I will swim or dive, she will find me, bring back the ball, give it to me, I will throw it . . . and then, of course, when I tire of the game (Billie is not supposed to get tired of the game) we quit, and I go back to writing or to watering.

Yeah, but old Billie won't drop the ball. She wants me to throw the ball, but she can't stand to give it to me first so that I can throw it. I want to throw the ball too, but she won't give it to me.

It's a standoff. I come up at the shallow end of the pool. I've swum three laps underwater easily—I'm trying for five, recapturing, as I do every summer, my youth. There's Billie, ball in mouth, a foot away. I reach. No deal. I go away a bit. She approaches. I come back. She retreats. I feign indifference. Then, old Billie, feigning indifference too, just lets go of the ball, which falls into the water, and she walks away from it, as if totally uninterested in it. She heads for the house.

The ball is now an inch from my nose, floating in the water. What shall I do? The whole thing runs against the eternal Rules for Dogs and Men (I don't want to hear anyone say, well, those are Men's rules: those rules are made by Dogs *and* Men).

Do I pick up the ball, or not? Well, it may be, it don't make a damn bit of difference. But if I'm as crazy and obsessed as she is, then I must refuse to pick up the ball, just let it float around there in the pool, teach her a lesson! maintaining that the Rules say she has to *bring it* to me, of her own free will. Otherwise, there ain't no game.

But I am not obsessed, I say to myself, and so I grab the ball. The instant I grab it, Billie Jean comes roaring out of wherever she was lurking and I fire the ball out into that part of the yard she's allowed to go in, and Billie rushes after it, grabs it in her jaws, rushes back to me in the pool and . . . and? well, we know that *she has learned her lesson,* lets me take the ball from her jaws, throw it, she chases it, brings it back, we'll now play ball from now on according to the rules . . .

It doesn't happen.

Billie Jean does not give me the ball. There has been no *transfer,* as some people I know are wont to say. The scene above has taken close to an hour to come to closure (same kind of word)—well, closure meaning when Billie Jean gives me the ball and I throw it, and Billie Jean gets to chase it, and we *understand* each other. That's what we're here for. From now until the next throw will take another hour. I give it up, and get out of the pool. I've got other things to do, man.

No sense of proportion.

I taught school for the first time in Heidelberg, Germany . . .

It's summertime. Summer vacation.

We do not call it *vacation* in the union—instead, it is a seasonal layoff. We have heard, all of us, all of our working lives, about as how we get two months' paid vacation and we are sick and tired of hearing it. We *don't* get paid, we argue. We get paid, poorly, we insist, for 180 days' work, and then get laid off, unpaid, the rest of the year.

(Then why not keep school open all year round? ask our nonteaching friends and critics, inevitably. You don't understand, we answer, rather weakly, and begin to change the subject.)

But it's still summertime, time to fool around with Billie, time, above all, to not-be working. Time to be writing about . . . schools, classes, teachers, students? But we teachers are not-teaching in the classroom, not-working, it's summertime and we can't be thinking about all that. It's all gone for now. (It will come back shortly.) I can't be thinking about drinking fountains or Chanh. The memories fade—the mind wanders. All to the good.

Thus, Heidelberg.

I didn't need a teaching job in Heidelberg at all. I was twenty-six. I *had* a job, and plenty else to do. I was working for the army as a postal clerk, moonlighted as a kind of doorman in a student jazz cellar, a so-called Cave, I had taken up playing the oboe and was practicing three hours, at least, every day . . . I particularly didn't need a job in a *school*.

I thought I had come to the end of the line with schools, back in Berkeley. Graduate school had made itself clear to me; you were now supposed to actually *do* something—*write* papers, *do* research, hell, do *something!* I had been quite content to listen to everyone in town, thus to learn, and later perhaps even to orate, agitate some myself, but this new requirement . . . I quit school and went to work in a small factory making a tool called a Shop-Smith, an all-purpose machine with a saw, lathe, and drill, which could do everything.

It was the first time that I had ever been not-going to school. (Well, a year and a half during the war, going to sea, but that was on account of the war. I mean, the first time without any excuse.) I was quite satisfied with the Shop-Smith job, and even more so with my new image as worker, which gave me a certain prestige, I thought, at campus political meetings among friends and enemies who were, after all, only *students*. In the end, however, I gave up this trade and sailed off to Europe, ending up broke in Heidelberg, where you could find a job at the American army headquarters.

The University of Maryland had an overseas division there, and ran, among other things, adult education courses for American army and civilian personnel. As it turned out, the person teaching one of these courses became ill, and went back home to America. The guy in charge of these courses was a frequent visitor to the jazz cave, and one evening asked me if I'd like to take over the course.

What course? History of Art. If there was any subject on earth that I knew nothing about, it was the history of art. That fact did not deter me, apparently, nor did the fact that

I didn't need a job or anything else to do. I look back on the whole thing with some astonishment.

Perhaps it is easily explained by the fact that, when I grew up, people were always offering you jobs, and you were expected to take them whether you wanted them or not (most often you did not, since these jobs always got in the way of going to the beach or something else important)—and you did. Still, it's interesting to see that I didn't think my utter lack of knowledge any particular handicap, nor my lack of any "teaching skills" and even less interest in any such thing. I wasn't, by the way, a total idiot in every way. It wouldn't have occurred to me, say, to stand up and play Haydn's Oboe Concerto in public, since I knew I didn't play well enough to do so then. Indeed, the first orchestra I played with, a small church group, wouldn't let me play at all, for fear of the distressing noises I occasionally made. I could rehearse with them, but in public I was just to sit there and look as though I was playing . . . the fact remains, I had no sense of the fact that I was proposing to stand up and talk to an audience for an hour on a subject about which I knew nothing.

I can only figure now that this bravery—or idiocy, or both—must have been the result of my experience as a student.

It was not totally true that I was an unserious student. We all read a lot, and certainly discussed what we read, plenty. It just always seemed to be that whatever I was reading, my classes were about something else I was not reading. If I was reading Lawrence, the class would be about Dryden. If I was reading Lenin, the class would be about Max Weber. I knew, from experience, that you could get through the class respectably without changing your reading habits at all, that is, without really knowing anything about it.

Accordingly, I went down to the Amerika Haus library and crammed just as I would have done had I been a student of art history facing a final. I looked at the textbook and the previous teacher's notes, saw where the class was, and went, the first night, armed with what seemed to me plenty of dope about Romanesque architecture, a word I had never heard of before. I also bought quite a few picture postcards of Romanesque churches to show—I mean, if the card said Romanesque, I had it.

Unfortunately, the moment I stood to address the class (in my experience, professors and teachers stood), I was struck down with stage fright. I had planned to read some from the text, but shook so violently that it was impossible. I had a neat little lecture all memorized, to be accompanied by the showing of my postcards, but could not hold on to the cards and had to get a young captain, actually my boss in the day-time, to hold them up. My lecture lasted not a half hour, but about ten minutes. I was out of gas. I recall apologizing. I was a little nervous—*a little?* my boss said to me the next day—assigned some pages to read and fled.

I had been in school all my life and just knew, almost un-consciously, what teachers did, that is, how they behaved while they taught. I had not planned on the stage fright. In the end, the class came out all right, I think. I talked with my boss and with the guy who'd offered me the job—actually I planned to quit—and began to get it about what was wanted in this class. The students were all officers and/or officers' wives, and what they wanted from the course was a little *Kultur.* I was in much the same boat. All of us had lived our lives in America within range of art museums, but had never entered them. Now, in Europe, we all went all the time, wherever we traveled, to museums, to cathedrals, and we wanted to know something about what we were looking at. We wanted to be able to say, this is Gothic, this Roman-esque, and how come it is, this picture looks like Breughel . . . nothing wrong with that, and once we got it straight, it worked OK. I collected more postcards, we drummed up an opaque projector, I read about the cards in the text and, while I never actually got over shaking, I could get the cards in the projector. These officers and their wives went somewhere every weekend, and they too brought back postcards and talked about them, what and when this was built, painted, by whom, taking over the class, which had now become something like a travel bureau or guide—go here to see this, there to see that, if you go to this town you'll see a fine example of this or that.

The class became something of a pleasure. After all, these officers and their wives were not *crazy*. They didn't want to go to school, for God's sake—just wanted to know something. Once I got over having to be a *teacher*, we were OK. I ended up with a fine postcard collection, and knew, in the end, quite a lot about what was to be seen in towns from Vienna to London, Amsterdam to Rome, and villages in between, although, in an odd turnabout, it was the students, not the professor, who went to all these places, since I was at once too broke and too busy to go running all over Europe.

It's only now, in summertime, that I think about it, and about my other teaching job the following year. What I want to say, I guess, is that I was very serious in those days about a number of things. I was serious about playing my horn, serious about improving my German and reading German literature, serious about learning something about European politics from the German university students at the cave, but I wasn't serious about schoolteaching, any more than I was about my job as a postal clerk.

I had never known anyone who was planning to be a teacher, no one who had ever taken an education course, and no thought about schools had ever entered my mind.

Had it, I think I would have seen the town of Heidelberg itself as a Good School.

11

Good Schools

"How much does the Empire State Building weigh?" Buckminster Fuller once asked a convention of architects in New York City.

I spent the summers of 1973, 1974, and 1975 at Mercer University, in Macon, Georgia.

American public schools were a source of discontent then, as now. Scholars and teachers and much of the public believed that the schools just weren't producing much in the way of serious learning—*real* learning—and that they had little respect for the intellect.

Of course, the reasons we gave for this lack were different then. The schools, those summers, were too rigid, too authoritarian, too bound up in rote memorization of isolated facts, too concerned with test scores, too disciplined; they were, most of all, "irrelevant" to the lives of the students of whatever age. In a word, they *promoted* ignorance and superstition, rather than combatted them.

Vietnam and the civil rights movement, counterculture—those had been the passwords. We had sought alternatives . . . to what? Well, to everything, in the end, but especially to the mind-numbing public school classrooms.

The only similarity to the present outcry was that then, as now, the *teachers* were to blame.

Mercer seemed to be an unlikely place for such a gathering as took place there those summers. A young education professor (and former power-lifting champion of the world) named Terry Todd got together one of the wilder collections of summer-school teachers and speakers yet seen under one roof. Besides well-known educators like Edgar Z. Friedenberg, John Holt, and Peter Marin, we had the farmer/poet Wendell Berry, Canadian free-schoolers, professors of Christian Ethics, blind folksingers, feminists, black school administrators from New York City, filmmakers, San Francisco poets, ex-linebackers for Texas football teams, behavior modificationists, musicians, and wild, tough veterans of southern civil rights and poverty programs, mostly ex-Baptist preachers under the mantle of the Committee for Southern Churchmen led by the redoubtable Will Campbell. "It got so," said Friedenberg, "I often thought that the speaker after me might come out wrassling an alligator."

All this at a small, private, conservative Baptist university in Macon, put together by the sheer willpower of Todd and the local power and political savvy of Joe Hendricks, another member of the Southern Churchmen and, then, assistant to the president of the university. Macon was a town where the mayor drove around in an army-surplus tank, which he later traded in for a navy patrol boat to cruise the Ocmulgee River in, guarding, in both instances, against revolution. The students were almost all regular Georgia public-school teachers, coming to the university as teachers will in summertime, to earn academic credits for promotion and salary. Some seemed pleased with one part of the show, some with another, some no doubt by none of it.

For me, it was a little Golden Age, but, as that age mostly involved coming to know people on the Mercer faculty who became lifelong comrades, the details can be left out. What is certainly true is that none of us had the slightest idea what to do about schools.

Well, not anymore. The "school movement" had been going on for quite a few years. Most of us there had been around free schools and alternative schools or taught delinquents to write poems in the park, taught drama in the jails of Canada, had run our own experimental schools in the public school system, or had established college classes without grades—professors at Mercer itself had a going, model Independent Freshman Program in which students designed their own programs and got credit for working in schools or mental hospitals, and Joe brought in genuine murderesses from nearby Milledgeville Prison to study on campus.

We had all done this stuff by the book, or at least by *our* books.

Our position was similar to that of a San Francisco State College professor who had convinced me of a number of progressive notions when I was getting my credentials, long ago (and perhaps caused me more trouble than I needed). I saw him on that campus, some years later during the riots there, shepherding a large group of Upward Bound minority high school kids through the college library. He was doing right, but he was not happy. The Upward Bound kids lived in college dormitories for the summer and were a source of unending trouble, he said. They were noisy, stole, broke into the Coke machines, and so on. I could see that, I told him, from the way they were roaming the library, pulling out card catalogues at random, laughing, yelling, spilling out the cards—if the idea was that making a leap with these minority ne'er-do-wells was going to imbue them with a love of learning, it wasn't working yet. Right, he said. I told my other education students just today that although my ideas are correct, they don't work!

That was more or less our experience, and our position. A letter from Todd to Friedenberg, published in *Katallagete,* the journal of the Southern Churchmen, sometime before these meetings, had made the point. Todd spoke of teaching at Auburn, not long before, doing right, being relevant, not grading, and so on, and had been pleased to hear from his students that they all thought his class the best they'd ever had, they'd all learned more than ever before, and it was an inspiration. He had been really excited, he wrote, until it came up one day, according to some schedule, that he could give the class a choice of going on learning all this wondrous stuff, or of having the day off. The class voted unanimously to have the day off.

That had shocked Todd a bit. My God! he thought to himself. Here we're having, by the students' own testimony, this wonderful educational experience, but they'd rather have the day off. He had wondered if Edgar could explain it.

Friedenberg had had much the same trouble. He had begun to teach, at Dalhousie University in Halifax, without giving grades, a fact accomplished, being as it was in Canada, with a good deal of personal struggle. Everyone was against it, especially the students, who thought that whoever *worked* ought to get better grades than whoever didn't. Edgar persevered though, perhaps telling the students they might like to learn for the sake of learning, rather than for grades. He got through the year, but the next year, his class swelled from thirty students or so to four hundred or so. Word had gotten around. Edgar's main insight was that he was getting ripped off.

By the summer of 1975, of course, even Todd could see that if he'd had any sense, he'd rather have had the day off too. Tom, purportedly a dean at Mercer, had hoped that the students, left to plan their own programs, would choose to read Plato and talk to him, Tom, about it. Tom, personally, thought a lot of Plato. Now he had begun to think, well, I'll just have to start again *making* these rascals read Plato. Tom *wanted* the rascals to read Plato.

Ted, a professor of something there at Mercer, had never thought that anything would work with the human race, but he liked very much the variety of the new programs, the fun, the talk, those *murderesses* and all, and, especially, that those programs seemed to be antiadministration, which afforded him pleasure, or so I think.

Everything we had thought of, and everything we had done, was right. Only it hadn't worked.

What was it that hadn't worked?

Well, the students had not all become scholars.

Was that what we had wanted? Was that the point of good schools, that everyone should read Plato?

We had begun to see that we had betrayed ourselves. We had all begun by arguing that the public school view of learning, of the intellect, was too narrow, bordered on the superstitious, and was oppressive. Our disappointment at how things had worked out seemed to mean that our ends had been, all along, just about the same. We hadn't been smart enough to ask ourselves, or the schools, some outrageous questions, like How much do schools weigh? in order to keep our own minds alert and wary.

As a cure, I, at least, tried to think of some good schools where things worked out just about right.

CHAPTER

12

Spring Training

I had a problem one spring, long ago, and solved it by creating a Good School.

Jay, my oldest son, was about nine, I think. He was recovering (if that's the right word) from encephalitis—or what the doctors guessed was encephalitis, since it wasn't anything else they could see—*anyway,* he'd progressed in a few years from not being able to move at all, just swallow and breathe, to crawling around and then tottering around standing up, to being able to run around a bit before falling down. What he wanted to do, above all, was to play baseball.

I thought that this was a good idea, to play a little ball, but the odds of doing so seemed against us. We lived about two blocks away from Helen Wills Playground, which had two asphalted ball fields, like all city playgrounds, so that was fine. What we didn't have was someone to play baseball *with.* Jay didn't want to just play catch, and couldn't at that time catch anyway. He wanted to *play baseball*—play a *game!* Hit, run, score, win or lose.

We had Jay, Jack, my younger son, about five, and me. Well, Jack would play. He would, at that time, do anything in order to be with his big brother. He seemed puzzled, I thought, about why his big brother fell down all the time, although he himself was only a year or so from falling down all the time too, but of course for a different reason. Still, Jay was a lot bigger and had muscles like iron from all the push-ups and other exercises he'd had to do since he was six, and he was Jack's official *big brother* even if Jay couldn't always talk right, and, well, that seemed to be enough.

Who to play *with?* There were plenty of kids playing ball down there at Helen Wills Playground, but they wouldn't do for us. They were eight, nine, ten . . . fourteen, but could *play,* and were out of our league. They would have been happy to play with us and slaughter us, but I couldn't have that.

You can always do something. We lived on the down side of Russian Hill, actually on the other side of the hill from North Beach. It had formerly been an all-Italian neighborhood, but the Chinese were even then buying into it. All the Italians said they would not, no never, ever, sell out to the Chinamen, no way; but of course when the Chinamen showed up offering cash money, they in fact did sell out and moved out to Tierra Firma, on the outskirts of town. Right where I worked and still work.

We were surrounded by Chinese families. All the Chinese adults, in those days, worked at least twenty-four hours a day. Our landlords did the same. We lived in this nice, old Russian Hill flat, six big rooms, paying ninety dollars a month, and over us the Chinese landlord and his family lived. The father was an engineer for the city. His wife ran a beauty shop in North Beach. Their two daughters went to U.C. Berkeley, studying, even then, engineering. After the father was done with his engineering job for the city, after the wife was done with her beauty parlor, after the girls were done with Berkeley, they all went down and attended to their laundromat. So they all got home about 11:00 at night and did then just what everyone else does in the morning, noon, or afternoon: they cleaned the house, vacuumed, made the beds, cooked dinner, did whatever they did. The girls had piano lessons at 12:30 A.M. and *practiced* early in the morning. I heard the first of Bach's "Two-Part Inventions" played, at 12:30 A.M., misplayed, started over again, bungled, and started over again, every morning.

So it came about that as I struggled with this problem of our ball team, as I went out on Saturday morning and looked around the streets hoping that the streets would solve all this for me, I could see all these little Chinese kids sitting stolidly on the steps leading up to their flats, formerly occupied by solid Italian families whose kids would have been out playing ball at Helen Wills Playground, no doubt. They were little kids; they ran from about four to perhaps ten. Boys and girls. They had been instructed by their fathers to sit there on the steps and not to move until the father or mother came home, some twenty hours later. They did so.

It took a day or two of seeing this, I guess, but I would now say that I saw *immediately* that these little kids were our ball club. I began to speak to them. I began to say, look, tell your father that we want to go down to Helen Wills Playground. I said, I'll look after you and bring you home, back to sit on the steps. I said, We'll play baseball! I was not confident that they understood.

I talked to our landlord about it, probably some day about 12:30 A.M. and he knew Jay and perhaps got it over to the Chinese kids' parents. However it was, one Saturday some ten or so of these kids left their stoops and gathered in our alley where we had a little batting and catching practice before heading out to Helen Wills Playground, marching down the two blocks and holding hands across the Broadway intersection.

We played work-up. There were three batters, one of whom

had to catch. When a batter was out, everyone moved up one position—right field to center, center to left, left to shortstop and so on (the out batter moved to right) so that eventually everyone got to hit. After everyone had hit, the game was over. How long that would be was up to me. I was, of course, the pitcher throughout the game. I was also umpire, manager, Owner of the Club, Commissioner of Baseball, and fan. It was a perfect position for any teacher to be in, and one of the reasons that it was a Good School.

It was also my job to keep the game going, keep the Chinese kids from being discouraged and heading back to their stoops. I keyed in, the first outing, on Jay.

Jay was bigger and taller than anyone else, and looked like a champ. After staggering up to the plate and tottering around a bit, he would get into his batting stance and stand there, solid as a rock, yelling at me to fire it in there. He had a perfect swing; level, even, elbows in, head up—he told me confidentially that he had copied his swing from Willie Mc-Covey.

In truth, I thought his swing *was* just like McCovey's. But its defect was that it had nothing to do with where the ball was; Jay swung the bat at the same level all the time. If the ball happened to hit the bat, if it was pitched exactly in the place where he swung, then *pow!* away it went.

Zeroing in on Jay, I began to understand how to gerrymander the game. I decided, for example, that Jay should mostly hit, otherwise he'd end up in the outfield or (good Lord!) on first base, where he would get killed by a hit or thrown ball. After he hit, though, there was another problem. He would tear down to first base, covered by a seven-year-old Chinese kid who immediately headed out of the way for fear of being run over by Jay, who then, experienced major-leaguer that he was, had to *make the turn* around first base. He invariably fell flat on his ass. It then took him a long time to get up and totter back to first, so by that time three or four Chinese kids in the outfield would have captured the ball and thrown it back somewhere and someone would get it and run toward first base to tag old Jay out!

I tried to talk Jay into just running past the base, slowing down, and taking his time getting back; "Don't make the turn," I'd advise him, "and then you're safe!"

He would tell me then that he had to make the turn in order to stretch his hit into a double, if possible. I cursed myself for having provided, at ball games or watching them on TV, this expertise. Moreover, it was obvious that with our fielders he could have stretched any hit into a home run, supposing he didn't have to fall down rounding every base making the goddamn turns.

You want to *hit,* I told him, and if these kids tag you out, then you can't hit!

When I fall down, he told me, then you call time out!

Once I got the idea, we had good ball games, lasting about two hours. I became, at long last, a great pitcher; I could hit the kids' bats as they swung, or not, as I chose. I could put them out or not. I could see which Chinese girls could catch—and let them make the putout—which kids couldn't, and make the putout myself when it was time for someone to be put out. I could even, finally, put out, or let Jay be put out, and let him take his position in right field, run down a ball, and throw it a long way, somewhere. Jack, at five and a half not being a professional ballplayer like Jay, could choke up, he said, on the bat, which was as big as he was, and hit it no matter where I threw it (not having copied Willie McCovey) and could catch besides, so I could let myself put him out from time to time and let him play first or right.

We played every Saturday, all spring. Who knows what major effect this game may have had on the structure of Western civilization?

After each game it became clear that we needed Popsicles. There was an Arab store right up the block from Helen Wills

Playground, and we would all gather round after someone made the last out and begin to discuss Popsicles. I was buying, as befitted the Commissar of Baseball, so that wasn't a problem; who would go get them, and what kind, was the problem. During the first games, kids argued about who got to go get the Popsicles and we had to flip endless coins which took half an hour. Looking back, and with all my experience *now* as a classroom teacher, I realize that the kids knew that whoever got to go get them would be assured of getting one, and of getting the kind they wanted, in case there was some mistake about how many, or even in case someone was to be *intentionally* left out. How did they know? I might be crazy . . .

By the end of our spring season, every kid knew there would be Popsicles enough, and no one wanted to trudge up one-half block to the Arab store and haul them back. It wasn't the work so much as that the job had become déclassé. Whoever went up was a chump and/or a flunky. Major-leaguers, even Chinese major-leaguers, didn't run errands. Major-leaguers wanted to sit around at Helen Wills Playground at the end of the game and brag. *I hit!* they planned to say. *I catch!* they would tell each other, while *someone else* brought them orange, lime, or grape Popsicles, according to their wishes, and their due.

In the end, I couldn't get anyone to go. Both Jack and Jay denied that they even *wanted* Popsicles. The Chinese kids, all of a sudden, didn't understand English. I was not equipped to say OK, No Popsicles at all. So I went up to the Arab myself. Well, I got even by buying a beer from the Arab and drinking it all by myself on the way back.

One problem was never solved in this Good School. There was this little wart of a kid, Win was his name (probably Wn, actually), and old Win, at perhaps seven, was playing on the team and lived three houses up from me. Win, like Jack, always hit the ball, no matter where I pitched it. That was OK, in terms of this ball game. Normally, I'd either field it and put him out at first, or field it, bumble it, let him be safe at first, or let it go past me and let the in-or-outfielders fool around with it, just like a real ball game.

But Win never bothered about what I did, or the infielders did, or the outfielders did. From the first game on, he hit—and then he ran to first, ran to second, safe or out, didn't matter to Win, and then kept right on going past second out through center field and out the gate of Helen Wills Playground and back to his home to sit on the stoop, and would never be seen or heard of again until next Saturday!

After the first game, I tried to explain to Win. OK, he said. Then he hit the ball, ran around first, ran through second and headed out the gate, and was never seen or heard of again until next Saturday, where he showed up, hit, and did the same thing.

I tried, in subsequent games, to strike old Win out just in order to keep him around, but couldn't do it. Wherever I pitched it, he hit it—maybe only a foot or two, maybe even just fouled it off. It was good enough for Win, and off he went.

On this last day, however, when I had to go and get the orange and lime and grape Popsicles, I kept one, and when we went back I went over to Win, sitting upon the stoop there, three houses away from mine, and gave him a lime Popsicle. That was the first time he'd ever gotten one, given his odd proclivity.

Win, I said. Next time you get to second base, just stay there. It'll be OK.

OK, he said.

13

Brim

One day near the end of our third summer at Mercer University, Arpine—who had been the reading teacher in our old alternative school-within-a-school at Spanish Main—and I received an invitation to come by Naropa Institute in Boulder on our way back home, and we agreed to do so happily.

On the way there, we stopped in Berea, Kentucky, to see our old comrade Jim Holloway, then professor of Christian Ethics at that university. We got out to his house in a little "holler." One thing clear about all southern professors is that they never live in town, but always out in some "holler," and, if possible, by some creek, and they all have forty acres or so. We sat up and talked and drank some and went to bed very late and in the morning Holloway had a little school set up for us.

We didn't know it at the time, of course. Next morning Holloway wanted to know if perhaps we would want to go a-fishing. As it just happened, he had a little pond down there full of fish, which *needed* to be fished, and maybe we'd . . . well, he had me, and so down we went in the morning. The pond was to be full of bass and crappie (called bream; pronounced "brim" in the South), and so I began casting out a lure into this little pond, planning to show Arpine that I knew all about fishing for bass and brim, but, of course, old Holloway had to butt in and tell me I wasn't doing it right and wonder where in the world I learned to fish and show me the *right* way—we did that for a bit. Shortly, I caught a little bass, and then Arpine cast and caught a bass, and so Holloway left.

We figured that was it for the day. We'd fish some, catch enough for dinner, and stop, be alone, then, talk, rest, nap, and so on. Fifteen minutes after we had demonstrated to Holloway that we at last knew what we were doing, and would do it, and were looking forward to doing it for a while, Patrick appeared.

Patrick was six years old; Holloway's son.

We entered a school immediately—it doesn't mean we were terribly pleased with that entrance, but we knew it and obeyed. Holloway had sent Patrick down to learn, from us, how to fish, and presumably, and much more important, that it was a good thing to do in yore spare time.

Well, we thought, it's Holloway's pond, his brim and bass, and his son. How come he needs us to instruct this kid? He didn't mind instructing *us,* did he? He knew how to fish the pond.

The point is, he knew everything—I believe you could say that about Holloway—but did not want to instruct his own kid in it, and therefore required a school. He was right. He knew that a school is a thing where your kid will be taught something which you could, of course, teach him yourself, if need be, but which you would rather someone else did. That's it about schools. What they are for.

In fact, since it was a *fishing* school, and since the bass and brim in the pond were reasonably willing, we had a pleasant morning. Patrick was an eager, sensitive student, only occasionally throwing rocks into the pond when the bites slackened. We caught enough fish for dinner and took them back to clean them, leaving Patrick, now accomplished, casting and throwing rocks into the pond. School was out for him.

Not entirely so, however, for us. Holloway came out to observe me cleaning the fish. I had learned to clean bass and crappie from my father, by the lakes of California, and had even, for a time, cleaned most of the fish we caught. I'll handle them, I would boldly say, while my father wondered aloud if I really thought I *could,* being a smart teacher himself. The image of being left alone with the sharp, sliver-thin cleaning knife, shoulder to shoulder with other fish-cleaning fishermen, talking about where you got *this* one, what lure pulled in *that* one . . . worked on me for quite a few years.

Times had changed. Now it was a chore. In any case, Holloway didn't watch long. He wanted to know where to God I learned to clean fish. I was too slick for Holloway, though, and wondered if he'd care to show me how he thought it ought to be done. He had to do it, of course, so I stood by with one of his beers observing his technique, admiring it, until Holloway got the notion and said he thought he *could,* after all, find another knife for me, if I wanted to help.

Arpine, in the meantime, had gone in to discuss cooking the fish with Holloway's wife, Nancy. Arpine wanted to sauté them just a bit in butter. Nancy thought that would be nice, but commented that Holloway would have a fit. They did it anyway, and Holloway came in and had a fit. He wanted those bass and brim deep-fried in egg and cornmeal and that was that. In the end, they cooked some one way, and some the other. Holloway didn't even glance at those sautéed in butter. I ate some of both.

So that was a Good School, if brief.

14

Naropa

We knew very little about Naropa, or what we were to do there. We knew it was some sort of Buddhist encampment. We knew that John Perks, a British guy who wrote me, was running some sort of summer school there at Boulder. We knew, because he said so, that Gregory Bateson would be there, and that is principally why we went, since Bateson was one of our heroes, although, talking about him on the airplane, we couldn't quite state why.

Oh, boy! What a school! Naropa appeared to be run by Chögyam Trungpa, a fugitive lama—in fact, by this time much of Boulder appeared to be run by him. Perks worked for him as a kind of majordomo. Trungpa was referred to as Rinpoche; we understood it to mean "enlightened." Bateson had apparently known and admired Rinpoche for some time. We were strangers to all this; we knew nothing about Buddhism, really, and certainly nothing of Naropa.

We ended up in a large, fancy sorority house, where school

was to go on, and the students and teachers housed. And what students! They were all, to my astonishment, young Ph.D.'s, mostly from the social sciences—anthropologists, psychologists, sociologists, all very successful, having done fieldwork in Africa, India, Ethiopia, and parts unknown, and published the results of their work, making it. What in hell were they doing back in school? They were the most successful, making-it lot I had ever seen in any school.

What a school! We sat there that first afternoon, Arpine and I, Perks, and Bateson, on the patio of this fairy-tale house, eating oysters, while the student Ph.D.'s stood inside pressing their noses against the window glass. These Ph.D.'s were not allowed to approach us. The difference between teachers and students was being made clear. Teachers ate oysters, or whatever Bateson, in fact, wanted. Students, eat whatever you can; we teachers are not interested in your problems.

I wondered some about our role in this school. Officially, it was the Educational Module of the Naropa Summer School. No one inquired of Arpine about the mysteries of teaching reading; no one asked me about discipline problems in the seventh grade. Perks had apparently read one of my books and liked it and thought I would be someone he'd like to talk to, a thought which turned out to be true. He told me about his life and Rinpoche's life and Buddhism and Gregory Bateson, and about the school he'd run once upon a time. He told me that, in order for things to look right (he was paying me out of Naropa educational money) I ought to give a lecture officially, and I did, but I thought it was a failure, mercifully very brief. No one was interested in the plight or problems of the public schools. The Ph.D. students didn't care; they had handled schools quite well. Perks and Bateson openly stated that schools were probably OK as they were, however they were. Perks remembered being made to memorize poems like "The Charge of the Light Brigade" and thought that was as good a thing to do in school as any.

Bateson agreed; they both thought that very few people learned anything anyway, that those who could learn would do so no matter what (an opinion Bateson was to repeat many times later on as a regent of the University of California), and so what the hell? Of course, neither one had ever attended any public schools, or not for very long.

After that, I settled in as teacher with nothing to teach and so had quite a pleasant and interesting time. This was the best school for teachers that I ever saw. We ate kidneys with Perks and Bateson in the morning, oysters in the afternoon. Cocktails at 5:00. Dinner was communal; someone was to cook each day for the school. Gregory made very good oxtail stew, ignoring the fact that most of the student Ph.D.'s were either vegetarians or aspiring vegetarians. We spent evenings listening to Denise Levertov, John Ashbery, and W. S. Merwin read publicly. We assembled with the rest to hear Rinpoche speak. This assemblage, not optional in the least, began at eight in the evening; Rinpoche always showed up at ten. We were told, upon wondering why the students fell for this every time, that students had indeed once gotten together and all showed up at ten—Rinpoche was there waiting for them, having been there since eight, and had prescribed quite a few unpleasant Buddhist penances. The students were all dressed in early seventies Ph.D.-hippie-Buddhist style with beads and hair and sandals and the rest; Rinpoche always showed up in Brooks Brothers attire, usually an immaculate safari shirt with epaulettes, beautifully tailored shorts, and knee-length stockings.

Well. We got the idea, somewhere along the line, that the students had become dissatisfied with their successful Ph.D. lives and, already having been through Freudian, Jungian, Gestalt, and nondirective analyses, having been to Esalen, having been rolfed and everything else they could think of or that had been suggested to them as The Way, they wanted to become Buddhists. Like all students they wanted everything—they wanted to remain Ph.D.'s, but they also wanted to be happy.

Gregory Bateson took over their instruction.

We went down with them to the creek. There they got pails of creek water, brought it back, and put it into an aquarium. Then we all walked down to a large vacant lot, surrounded by parking lots, where Bateson pointed out the existence of prairie dogs. He gave instructions; they were each to spend six hours daily lying flat on the ground observing the prairie dogs. They were to write down everything they saw. It was over 100 degrees outside; there was no shade. After that, they were to come back and spend any free time they had looking into the aquarium water with Bateson's magnifying glass, and were to write down and draw everything they saw. That was it.

Nothing was said about what to do with these notes and drawings. The rest of the time they were free to "sit" (the Naropa term for meditation) or make love, as Perks strongly suggested they do, or learn to play poker or shoot dice with me in the evenings. Perks thought me perfectly suited for this kind of instruction (the only error I thought he made) and bought a bottle of bourbon whiskey (with school funds) which he apparently thought appropriate for this subject. I became the target of Ph.D.'s trying to do what they were told, shooting dice and crying out, "Little Joe!" and "Nina from Pasadena!" if they were trying to get four or nine.

Bateson gave a lecture, talking for about two hours to the effect, I think, that the world went to hell with the invention of language, which had separated humans from the rest of the universe and was an altogether bad thing. He wanted to discuss how to get back to that primal state. We all sat, fascinated; we understood very little, I believe—still, we were fascinated. A guy talking about getting rid of talking by talking . . .

Perks gave a lecture and slide show about his own experi-

mental school, apparently a few years back, one supported
by some sort of state funding in New York. Perks had, he
said, spent most of the funds for longboats, eighteenth-
century uniforms, and a *cannon;* he showed slides of the students cruising the river and the coast in these boats, firing off
the cannon, led by Perks himself in the role of Captain Horn-
blower. I felt a terrible pang, seeing this—why couldn't I
have known Perks when alternative schools were the rage?
Perks was clearly the real thing . . .

That was it. It was an entirely different aspect of the Good
School.

Arpine was actually interested in the prairie dogs and in
the aquarium water and often accompanied students to the
vacant lot and gazed through the magnifying glass. Being on
the staff, though, she could quit whenever she wanted. I made
a little money off the dice-shooting students, had a fine time
eating oysters and kidneys, and was very happy listening to
Bateson, Perks, and the poets. (Bateson, it ought to be said,
was ill at the time, but he was always extremely kind and
gracious to the students once they had done their chores. He
met them, talked with them, listened—gave his time constantly. He only refused to tell them what they were doing.)

The students? I guess the virtue of the place for them was
that they were doing as they were told—nothing unusual in
itself for students who have become Ph.D.'s!—but doing it
either for no reason at all, or for some reason they couldn't
understand, or for no apparent benefit to themselves. That
must have been new to them, and seemed to suffice. After all,
they had come to the end of the line, somehow, an end considered to be wonderful by all schools of my acquaintance up
until then, but which had not contented them and which was
currently seen to be worthless.

When we left, Perks told me that Rinpoche was going to
make a trip out to the West Coast soon and then Perks and I
could go salmon fishing.

Perks was eager to fish and said he thought he could get a dispensation from Rinpoche which would allow him to do that, if I would guarantee to bait his hook for him and remove any fish he caught from his hook. Just so he did not touch the *killing instrument,* he said.

I had a brief vision of Perks and Holloway, down at Holloway's pond, and wondered if that would be a Good School or not.

CHAPTER

15

Black Mountain

I left Berkeley, one summer while I was still an undergraduate, to go to the famous Black Mountain college in North Carolina. I was twenty-two or twenty-three, just a boy, and had just begun to know everything.

I did not know much about its fame then, but I was friends with two painters who had been there and who were going back. The reason I went was because some older painter, from Chicago, had a house down on the Yucatan Peninsula and we were all going to meet up with this guy in Black Mountain and go down there to live. They had pictures of the house to prove it—it was wonderful. Right on a beautiful beach, palm trees, jungly—I don't know about them, but I had a hundred dollars and I planned to go down there and never come back.

Well, the deal fell through. The painter from Chicago had been offered a one-man show and couldn't make it and perhaps had decided to rent out the place instead, or it really wasn't his; and one of the painters I knew was offered a job teaching at Black Mountain that summer. I was very angry, and so, although I stayed at Black Mountain all summer, I continued to resent it and resist its charms.

Black Mountain had two heroes in residence that summer. One was the poet, Charles Olson. He was a huge man, and perhaps a little domineering, or perhaps it was my own resentment at fate which led me to avoid him.

The other was Buckminster Fuller. We heard the story when we arrived. Fuller had engaged the students in building his geodesic dome, a common enough term now, but not then. Indeed, it was supposed to have been the first one ever constructed, outside of tiny models. Fuller had told the students that the dome, some sixteen feet in diameter, was an antigravity machine. They were going to put it together, he said, and then some twenty of them were going to pick it up, lift it about a foot into the air, and *the dome was going to stay there,* held off the ground by the energy structure of those triangles, or something.

They did it, but naturally, the dome just fell back to earth, where it still stood.

That story suited my mood, and I sneered at the gullible Black Mountain students.

When Fuller left, a few days later, I scoffed even more openly. He was trying to pack his stuff into a small trailer. Fuller had made a number of models of this and that, all of them from Ping-Pong balls attached together by wooden rods, in a great variety of shapes and forms. Every time Fuller got the trailer packed, he would look around and one or two of his Ping-Pong ball structures would be still left out, and wouldn't fit. After an hour or so of this, Fuller flew into a rage. There was quite a group of us sitting around in the grass watching him pack—mostly poets and painters who had become his architecture students, waiting to say good-bye and talking about what a genius he was. Fuller stopped his packing and gave us a sermon. He had brought all these Ping-

Pong balls and wooden rods *down* here in *this* trailer and they were, by God, going *back* in *this* trailer! He cursed the inventor of trailers for having made them in this stupid, un-yielding shape! He reprimanded the rigid minds of men! He denounced the structure of the universe, which made trouble whenever he, Fuller, rearranged it in the slightest!

In the end he stormed back into his house. His wife came out and packed up the trailer; perhaps she had to dismantle a few models in order to do so. After a bit Fuller came out too, and they drove off.

This tantrum made me very happy, as you may imagine, because I could see I didn't have to worry about having been wrong about this silly joint. That made it a Good School.

Of course, later on it became clear that even if the geodesic dome wasn't an antigravity machine, it had plenty of other virtues and its builder, Fuller himself, became famous. I had, certainly, to take back and even eat my sneering words— another facet of the Good School.

— **16** ——————————————————

Gary and Alfred

"No Good Deed Goes Unpunished."

Back at Spanish Main School. One afternoon, just after school was out, Gary came into the teachers' room. As it happened, only Arpine, David, and I were still there. Perhaps we were talking about some outrage—that's what we usually talked about. Gary entered with that air he always has when he has something extraordinary to relate. He comes in, advances a step or two, and stands, waiting for us to give him our attention.

We give it. He reaches into his pocket and pulls out something, conceals it in his right hand. We wait.

What would you guess this is? he asks us. Without waiting, he says, This is *one thousand dollars!* I just took it off Alfred Stone!

Whoa! What? A thousand dollars? A *grand!* . . .

Gary goes on to tell. Well, we all know Alfred, Arpine and I had him in the seventh grade, he reminds us. Sure we do.

Alfred is an eighth grader; he is troublesome and disruptive, all the time. Not mean, violent, or vicious. He's a nice kid, but troublesome. That's what drives us nuts. He won't conform. He won't do his homework or classwork. He won't shut up. Won't come for detention for not shutting up. Arpine has to remind us that he is a good reader. It seems that every time we bring up some troublesome kid, Arpine tells us that he or she is a good reader. We don't want to hear it, in the face of that thousand-dollar roll, which Gary now shows us. He counts it for us—a roll in twenties and fifties.

The main thing we know about Alfred is that he will steal anything not nailed down. He is famous for it. He is the original kid about whom teachers are always exclaiming, Why should he remain in school? Don't we have any standards at all?

Gary goes on. I'm on lunch duty, he says, and I always just kind of keep an eye on Alfred anyway, just watch him roam around looking for something to steal, but now I see him over in a corner of the multiuse room surrounded by a bunch of kids, a big bunch of kids, which is unusual. I sidle over there. Usually when I come over, the group breaks up—whatever it is they were up to, they know I won't like it, so they just split. This time, they're too excited or interested to break up. They don't even notice me. When I get there, I see Alfred handing out money, bills, to every kid in sight! Now that's what you call unusual!

Then they see me, of course, and all suddenly have business elsewhere. I confront Alfred. I discuss with him, briefly, about why he is giving out money. It's rather out of character, to say the least. In the end, I prevail on Alfred to pull out this roll—well, I have to threaten him just a bit—and here it is! One thousand bucks! And that's only what he had left!

We all fall back. I told him, Gary says, to just keep cool and not say a thing, told him to go into my P.E. office after school and just stay there, while I figure out what to do. He's there now. I just looked in, being it's Alfred, and saw him. Stay put, I told him. He said he would.

Well, hell, now, says Gary, we all know that Alfred is a cold crook, but he's supposed to be a minor-league crook, taking quarters that girls left in their desks, maybe conning or bullying a kid or two out of their lunch money, but a *thousand dollars?* Up until now we all had hope for him, right? He's a smart kid (Gary nods to Arpine), and we all plan to straighten him out, right?

Its true. We do.

But if he gets caught . . . *wait,* we all say, what do you mean, *caught?* You already caught him, Gary . . .

But we know what Gary means. If we had been sympathetic to Alfred before, now we are unexplainably even more so. Possession of a grand will get Alfred right into the pokey. All of a sudden, none of us wants that to happen.

Gary sits down then, and we discuss it. We don't know what to do, so at first we all jive around, splitting up the grand four ways among us, and telling Alfred to shut up or it's off to the jug. We know that we just ought to call the cops; we ought to just tell the principal, Dave, at this time, and let him handle it, call the cops, whatever. What is Alfred to us?

Hell, we finally say, the thing to do is to talk to Alfred, find out where he got this dough, talk to whomever he got it from, and try to give it back without making a fuss. Talk the guy, whoever he is, into it, and then we'll have reformed Alfred! He'll recognize the seriousness, etc. . . .

These three have since blamed me for having made this suggestion, but I deny it.

We agree that Gary and David (who is, after all, a special ed. teacher, supposed to know how to counsel crazy kids) will go talk to Alfred now. That's what they do.

They come back, triumphant. Alfred is still in the gym, for one thing; a good sign. So Alfred told Gary and David that he was just down, just before lunch (so *cutting school,* damn him!) at a little hamburger and coffee shop just off the shopping center—a block or so from the school.

What for, Alfred? they asked him. Were you going to buy lunch there? No, just looking around, he told them. Then he just happened to see, on the counter, a gray bank bag which he, Albert, recognized as being the kind of bag which businesses used to place their cash deposits into the bank. (We shuddered. We would not, we told each other, have recognized that.)

Alfred said he figured someone from the coffee shop was to pick up this bag full of deposits and take it over to the bank, also only about a block away. So, *on impulse,* he just picked it up, took out the money, and, being the sort of nice guy he was, began giving out twenty-dollar bills to friends of his at lunchtime.

Gary and David then said that they had talked old Alfred into giving the money back; he had supplied a partial list of friends to whom he had given twenty dollars.

Gary and David had then, *insanely,* as they admitted later (after blaming me for the whole idea), decided that all they had to do was to find the bank bag, put the roll back in it, put it back on the counter of the coffee shop, and that would be it, *fini, c'est tout!* So? So Alfred had told them that he had run around the back of the coffee shop and took out the money and thrown the bank bag into a Dempster Dumpster, which stood at the back of the shop.

We all forgot about the twenties Alfred had given away, in our urge to put everything right. It was decided that Gary, and Gary *agreed,* would go down with Alfred to the Dumpster, find the bank bag, and we'd go from there.

Gary went off to get Alfred. We, David, Arpine, and I, sat there, waiting. We talked about Alfred; we convinced ourselves that we were doing right.

We talked about doing right for over an hour. Finally,

Gary came back. He got our attention again. He was not pleased.

You can all imagine, Gary said, just about how pleased I am to be rummaging around in garbage for an hour or so!

He went on to tell us about it.

Son of a bitch! he said. So we got there, we *snuck* back of the coffee shop. We're both guilty now, you got to see that. I hadn't figured on that, but of course we both are, Alfred's a crook and I begin to realize I'm abetting his ass. The whole thing is Jim's fault—*he* suggested it.

Alfred had pointed out the correct garbage bin, the Dumpster, and Gary found himself rummaging around in that bin. He noticed that Alfred stood to the side, not entering into the search at all. Alfred, so Gary said, didn't plan to rummage around in any garbage pail. He was above that. Gary couldn't see the bank bag.

So finally, Gary said, outraged, mad as hell (how come I had to be doing this? he asked Heaven and so on, blaming all of us, especially me), so finally, I got *in* the motherfucking Dumpster! I got *in* it, climbed *in* this garbage, wallowed around in it, while Alfred is just leaning up against the fence, not participating at all, watching me wallow around— you know that if I could ever really hate anything, it's wallowing around in garbage! Alfred is not in here looking for the goddamn bank bag. He ain't doing shit!

The bank bag isn't in there. I crawl out. I'm planning to kill Alfred. He's cool, *insouciant.*

Alfred, Gary says he says, crawling out of the garbage bin, *I don't find the bank bag!*

Well, Mr. Riley, says Alfred, just leaning up against the fence, cool, perhaps I made a mistake. Perhaps I didn't really throw it in there. Maybe I even didn't find it, didn't even *find* the money, there. Not *there,* in that joint. Maybe.

Gary is going crazy. Gary says he has decided that maybe we aren't going to reform Alfred.

Jesus! We agree. Alfred may be out of our league, after all. Alfred has been sent home to his mama, so says Gary. Gary will not kill *us,* we hope and trust. We go in and tell Dave, the principal, still around at this late hour. He is not pleased with us. We have principals here! he says. We slink out, guilty, not knowing if we have principals or principles.

The investigation is thus out of our hands. The principal will have to handle it. As time goes on, Gary does not get over it; *your idea,* he tells us, got *me* crawling around in that garbage can!

All I know is, he says, that as long as I live I've got this image, this picture of myself crawling around in that garbage can like an idiot, looking for a bank bag that Alfred *knows* isn't there in the first place! Alfred *knows* it!

In the end—well, it was never totally clear—Dave remained annoyed with us and we never quite got the full story. The owner of the café had not lost any bank deposits. It finally appeared that Alfred's mother, or his mother's boy friend, or both, had "picked up" the money from a furniture store in another town entirely and that Alfred had "found" it at home weeks later and brought the roll to school. Alfred himself was soon back being troublesome and a good reader. His mother seemed to have wiggled out of it. Those who suffered, besides Gary, seemed only to be a number of seventh and eighth graders who got in considerable trouble with their parents after the cops explained that the kids had received stolen goods and that the cops wanted the ten or twenty bucks back. Naturally, the kids had spent the money on candy or cigarettes or baseball caps—without telling their parents, and so they got grounded or beaten or both. Gary said that a number of them, understandably bitter, threatened to get together and beat Alfred up, but nothing ever came of it.

17

Some Fast Learners

Before I left Heidelberg I had another teaching job. This job was in a small base in Schwetzingen, nearby, where the army had established a GED (general equivalency diploma) program. The army had decided that it was going to be a literate army; noncoms without high school educations/ diplomas were going to get them, or stop being noncoms. Experienced teacher that I was, I was hired to teach these noncoms in high school English, math, history, and science. We had class two days a week, two hours a day, for sixteen weeks, at the end of which all were to take the GED test. All did take it, all passed it, and all possessed forever after the equivalent of a high school diploma.

The students were almost all sergeants, aged from twenty or so to fifty years old, most had left school before the sixth grade; all could, however, read and write reasonably well, and all wanted to continue being sergeants, rather than be busted back to PFC.

At the time, of course, I didn't think about it, but later on, when I did wonder why it was they all passed easily, that seemed to be it—they had some real reason to. When I thought about it, much later, I found it rather surprising that sixteen weeks, twice a week, had sufficed for these students to "learn" (pass a test about, anyway) material that schools found it necessary to give *twelve years* to, and even then many kid students found this material too difficult!

The question is, of course, what was it that was surprising? That the army students passed it? That many kids don't after twelve years? Did it mean that if the kids didn't go to school at all until they were eighteen, then went for a few weeks with some reason to do it, that they would all pass? All be educated? Free of ignorance and superstition?

Those kinds of questions plagued educators then (although not me) and plague them now, it seems. Since then, hundreds of studies and books and reports have been written to show that if kids don't go to school at all, they end up, on average, just about as educated as those that do. What no one can figure out is why my sergeants, had they actually *gone* to high school, would have been unable to pass the test, a fact that is almost 100 percent certain. It is probably this uncertainty—this *worry*—which causes all the swings of the pendulum that so concerned me earlier on in this book.

One last note on the past; when I first took an actual teaching job, in a real, live public high school up in the mountains, in the gold country of California, I was supposed to teach art, along with English. That happened because they needed an art teacher, because they had art down as a subject in the curriculum, and here I came with History of Art at the University of Maryland on my resume! What could be better? But as it happened, even though I was no longer shaking with fright, my postcards and opaque projector captivated no one. No students were traveling to the city to go to the museums. Romanesque versus Gothic arches could not be sold.

These real high school students wanted to *paint* and *work in clay!* Down I fled, once again, to Fine Arts in the city to see painters and craftsmen to find out the difference between water colors and gouache, what kind of clay, what to do with it, what kind of paper to buy, how much paint, brushes . . .

PART III

Opening Day

"Jaybirds are not Archangels!" the late poet Jack Spicer used to state. He usually meant, by that phrase, to deflate some overpompous demand or claim—say, that Art or the Socialist party would save the world.

Still, I always thought he meant, too, that if not Archangels, jaybirds were still jaybirds, thus not a bad thing to be at all, and did a good job of being jaybirds.

CHAPTER

18

Collective Bargaining

But summertime has fled.

I know it has, because the phone begins to ring. It rings about negotiations, about the budget and its "ending balance," and about hiring and firing and transfers of administrators and teachers. It seems as if none of this has been far from anyone's mind during summertime.

Everything is fine at first. A caller tells me that the new board of trustees (hereinafter "board") has fired three principals and a few administrators. Sent them back to the classroom! On the recommendation of Dave, the superintendent!

Another tells me that the board had an "ending balance" of over a half-million dollars. All right! That's our raise for next year, signed, sealed, and delivered! The new board is doing right!

There are many more such pleased calls, especially about the administrators. It is nothing personal, in most cases. Well, in some cases it is. It is simply that we all, we teachers, feel that the district has too many administrators, that they are not needed, don't do anything much, have too many assistants, too many secretaries, get in our way, make rules which hinder us, spend the money we need for supplies, and in the end ought to go back to the classroom and work.

Many of us, I regret to say, worked in Tierra Firma twenty years ago. Then we had double the number of kids, double the number of teachers, but only one-quarter the number of administrators. The good old days! you can hear us saying. We add up the state and federal "programs" which over the years have added to the administration: ESAA (to cure us of racial prejudice) for which we got credits on our salary schedule for going to Chinese restaurants or listening to Spanish tunes, ESL, bilingual ed., Miller-Unruh reading, Title I or Chapter-This-and-That, Resource Programs for the lowest "percentile," the expansion of special ed. . . . each program with its own director and supervisor and assistant and secretary, all viewed with some suspicion.

WPA for administrators! we cry, if we are old enough.

I went to school as a kid not knowing a *word* of English! we cry if old enough and (in this town) Italian enough.

And money! Our first year of negotiating we bargained for a 12 percent raise and a good three-year contract. A victory for the union on our first shot at it! Well, next year just 6 percent, but—a big *but,* a signed pledge by the board to put in more if they had any money left over. This was a new board, newly elected, going to right the many wrongs of the old board, and especially planning to support teachers, many of whom had campaigned for them in Tierra Firma.

So the half-million left over was great! Union and teachers were in business!

Me too, I figured, abandoning summertime completely. I began to talk on the phone a lot, and with some pleasure, two weeks before school started.

Abruptly, the tone of these calls changed. What? The sons

of bitches . . . we knew . . . too good to be true . . . can't trust . . . goddammit!

What went wrong? The president of the old, evil board had once been overheard (it was reported) to say, going into negotiations, Let's go tease the teachers! The new, good board had changed all that, we figured.

All of a sudden, the phone said, the board took it all back. They rehired all directors and supervisors and principals. They said they *couldn't* give the money for salaries, since they were afraid they would go bankrupt if they did. They allowed as how they'd probably have to lay off teachers. One week later, everything had changed.

Holy Christ! said the phones. What went wrong? Well, these decisions had been made on Dave's recommendations. The board had apparently forgotten that one of the wrongs they planned to right included Dave. They considered him to be a villain, a puppet of the old board. They hoped to fire him. Thus, perhaps they remembered that if Dave recommended these moves, sensible as they seemed, the moves must be wrong. In the meantime the business manager had quit (in a conflict with Dave, everyone said) and so the budget was being made and approved and figured out by Dave too, and so the board remembered again that they didn't trust Dave, who they decided probably *wanted* the district to go bankrupt so the new, good, reform board would look bad. Since they had no expertise or even the slightest idea about the budget themselves, they had no place to go, no way to turn.

Note that earlier "hereinafter." I have become a schoolhouse lawyer. I have a different kind of call. It is from an upset teacher, who has been told that she is being summarily transferred. No one ever wants to be transferred.

Who told her this? Well, the principal, of course. Principals still tend to forget our contract, or hope we'll forget, one or the other. They prefer to just say, You go and You stay without reference to our legal, signed, rather complex (they say) but *fair* (we say) procedures for transferring teachers.

I call the principal. He's already at school working (and transferring people) according to his contract. We've still got another week. What's this? I want to know. He's surprised that there is a problem. I get the notion that he feels I'm butting into his business at his school with his teachers. We go over the question of transfers. He's a sensible guy, and doesn't cause any trouble. OK, he says, I know it. I just thought that I could transfer her because she wouldn't complain.

Well, she did complain, I say. We agree to work it out. No problem, I tell the teacher. Three days later she calls to tell me she wants to transfer after all. She doesn't want the principal to be mad at her, because he might *harass* her. No, he won't, I say. The union . . . etc. She goes anyway. The next call is from another teacher who says he *heard* that the teachers of that building, all with phones, say that the union let one of their colleagues be transferred unfairly!

Hell! School hasn't even begun! I give up and go to the school board meeting. It's only three days (not counting the weekend) before school starts up. Board members are arguing about rehiring resource and ESL and Title This-and-That teachers before final funding by the state or the feds. What if we go bankrupt? some say. We have to have these programs by law! others recall. What to do? Wait for funding. But school begins Tuesday!

I remind the board they wait too long every year to rehire the teachers, that every year the funds come in as promised, that every year the board members then complain that these programs didn't get started in time. Why not try it the other way around for once? I say. Well, that is just the union talking, which doesn't care if the district goes bankrupt and certainly doesn't have the responsibility, I'm informed.

I'm still out here with Billie Jean and the pool and the warm weather (twenty degrees warmer than Tierra Firma, although only thirty miles away) but I drive in again to talk to Dave. We've always gotten along very well in our union/superintendent relationship. He's proud of the fact that we've had no official grievances, that we've worked them out together, no Unfair Labor Practices, no slowdowns, informational picketing, or like troublesome activities. I feel that Dave, although hiding money in the budget all the time, has come through with the money in the end, by some timetable of his own that I don't have to understand. Now Dave is even coming close to being known as the teachers' friend, he believes. Well, I observe to myself that he has a long way to go; our memories are long. Also, the new board is or was supposed to be good, making Dave, a product of the old, no-good board, bad all over again.

Dave is suing the new, good board, he tells me, swearing me to secrecy. What for? For not following my recommendations, he says. It's against the law! He goes on to explain why.

What about this money? I say. Goddammit it, Dave, what about the half-million?

He tells me it's needed to balance next year's budget. He tells me what a jerk the old business manager was. I'm beginning to feel nervous. This ain't going to work out nicely.

I tell Dave he's got to come through with the money. I figure he will, as usual, in a while. Well, I try to believe that.

Before the next board meeting, the phone rings a hundred times to tell me the secret: Dave is suing the board! At the board special meeting, however, the board is back discussing the gardening contract, still under suspicion, and their problems with classified employees and *their* union about who is to clean out gutters before the rains come and flood everything. None of this is new.

Bottled water is now under discussion. One board member claims that if the administration building is to have bottled water, then the schools must have it too.

I think fleetingly of the life expectancy of bottled water

on its little stand in Spanish Main Junior High. One year, long ago, we experimented with a pay phone in the cafeteria. Once again with a jukebox. Ten minutes, they lasted. Maybe fifteen seconds for bottled water . . .

I write a note to the school whose teachers claimed the union was letting them be transferred unfairly. We can't have this going around, especially since it's not true. I remembered that these teachers at this school mostly don't even belong to the union, don't pay dues. Naturally, they complain and naturally are ignorant.

I get a call from the board's negotiator. She calls from a place four hundred miles away. Her name is Candace.

"Call me Candy," she says, very friendly.

OK. I suggest we begin negotiating right away, settle this problem of money—a minor one, I imply—and get to work on our new, three-year contract. I foresee no difficulties, I say.

The board has not instructed her to negotiate, she tells me, coldly. Besides, she is off to North Dakota or somewhere on business.

The next day I get a letter from Call-Me-Candy saying that the board is making a last and final offer, which is just a bonus. Pennies! Not on the salary schedule! I write back, outraged; I explain our position in the county (bottom). I declare she can't give us an ultimatum without ever seeing us, the budget, without ever meeting . . . I mention unfair labor practices.

The rest of our negotiating team is equally outraged. We've been sitting around for some time, hearing negotiators tell us they "have no instruction." We show figures, we've analyzed the budget, we have graphs, scattergrams, we know the salaries of every other district in sight, we've done our homework, we have this *signed pledge,* we have the *ending balance,* we know the state has handed out a 6 percent cost-of-living-adjustment for next year (and I'm reduced to talking like that, in terms of COLAs and such!), and by God . . .

By God. We're not putting up with it. We call the newspapers. We meet together and drive each other crazy with the question, What are we going to do?

There are Arpine, Gary, Dolly, Karen, and Dorothy. Our anger at the negotiator and the new, good board gets turned against each other. Why don't I do something? Protest! Organize demonstrations! Call the governor. Sick-outs! Slowdowns!

We recall the good old days two years ago with Slick, the first negotiator for the district. Districts usually hire lawyers who specialize in labor relations to negotiate for them. Unions usually don't. We do it ourselves, with the aid of state field representatives to figure out the parts where the lawyer-expert is trying to outsmart us. Maybe we send the final contract to *our* lawyer to take a look at the language, again to guard against legerdemain.

We began to like Slick quite a bit after the 12 percent raise, and we could see that he'd helped us out some on the contract, reminding us of things we forgot, showing us how to write it down so that it meant, legally, what we wanted it to mean, at least in places where he didn't care about the article in question. It is one of the best contracts in the whole state. We called him Slick fondly, and took photographs together when we finally came to agreement on the contract and got it neatly printed up in a little blue booklet.

By the next year we were saying Slick in a different tone. It took us most of the year to get to our 6 percent, much of the time with that damn Slick saying he had "no instruction" from the board. It took a long time for Dave to dig out the money he'd hidden, and it wasn't enough. Then the damn board, the new, good board, reneged on its pledge! We wanted Slick to do something about it. We began to think fondly of the old, bad board.

Abruptly, the board too got tired of Slick and wanted to

fire him, although we never knew why. Perhaps they thought once again that he was in league with Dave. Slick, however, sent in another man from his firm.

Mad as we were at Slick, Little John fared worse. He *never* had any instructions! Where Slick would at least pretend to blame the board for this (another reason to fire him, perhaps) Little John didn't even do that.

Then too, Little John told us the kind of stories that no doubt every negotiator tells, a stock-in-trade, perhaps, perhaps page one in the *Negotiator's Handbook,* but we had already heard them from Slick. Heard them, been impressed at first, being novices—but we were in our third year at the table, we knew it all, and we didn't want to hear these stories again from Little John.

You see, he'd say, this is the analogy. (We immediately knew he was going to tell us why the board, with all this obvious money, couldn't afford a raise.)

Say you want to buy a car, he went on.

We groan. Holy Christ, Little John, we already heard that one! He goes on.

Say you want to buy a car, and it costs two hundred dollars down. All right, say you've got the two hundred. So you put the money down, and own the car, but you forgot to allow for the fact that you had to pay the two hundred dollars every month! You don't have it every month! You only had it the first month. You see? That's the position the board is in. They can't pay the raise every month for this year. Don't you see . . . what would you do?

Well fuck it! Gary tells him, driven mad by this.

We already heard that tale!

But what would you do then? asks Little John, certain he has an airtight case.

Do? shouts Gary. *Do?* I'll tell you what—I'll *buy the goddamn car* and if I can't pay for it next month, they can just come around and *repossess* the son of a bitch! That's what I'd do!

Now we have Call-Me-Candy, whom we haven't even seen, giving us this ultimatum. What happened to the good board? What happened to good, old Slick, and (now) good, old Little John?

What happened to good, old so-and-so, the former business manager who quit?

What's happening to Dave? Now Dave is retiring, he tells me. What? He's not putting up with this crazy school board. He doesn't need it, he says. But now the board, who wanted to fire Dave, said they did, refuses to let him quit before his contract is out in a year or so and they get the D.A. to write Dave letters forbidding him to, we hear . . . what the hell is going on?

We organize a big demonstration at the board meeting. We've got three hundred people there, teachers, parents, clerical employees—we make speeches, neatly orchestrated, we get in the newspapers: TROUBLE IN TIERRA FIRMA! Nothing happens, though. Call-Me-Candy stands pat. The board doesn't move.

We'll recall the assholes! cry teachers. I remember that in this town of eighty-five thousand, only eighteen hundred voted for the school board. A recall just might not work. Anyway, I remind people, most teachers supported these guys against the old, bad board. In fact, most of the old, bad board were supported by teachers against an earlier old, bad board. Who have they got waiting for us next . . . ? Sick-outs, slowdowns, picketing, strike! Goddammit, the union is not doing anything . . .

Call-Me-Candy finally meets with us. Perhaps the demonstration worked, perhaps the publicity influenced them. We don't know . . . Call-Me-Candy has no new instructions from the board. In their meetings, the board is fighting with the Personnel Commission. They are discussing the problems of gutters. The rainy season is coming, they point out to each other. They are not discussing our negotiations. Dave has taken his vacation and will take all his sick leave to boot, he says. He has some two hundred days of it. We have no business manager. Now we have no superintendent. The board has no notion of what to do and is not paying any attention to us anyway . . .

At the table, Call-Me-Candy begins to tell us a story. It is exactly the same story that good old Slick told us at our first bargaining session, that good old Little John told us . . .

Well, this is all interesting no doubt, and perhaps exciting, and it continues, even as I write. But wait! We are, all of us, schoolteachers, and the funny thing is that school has started for another year.

19

Opening Day

I began this with a Friday, June 17, the last day of school for that year. The school season, like that of baseball, is strictly set and once set, can't change. No more times at bat after closing day. Off-season—for us, summertime—is to do something else; fish, sell real estate, work out, rest injured arms and psyches. Very shortly after Labor Day, for us, the season will begin all over again. Opening Day it says, right on the school calendar. It is September 7.

Well, what do we do here, now that school is starting once again?

I go get my room key. I receive a lot of other stuff too—I get a note from a teacher who is outraged because we aren't getting a raise and what is the union going to do about it? I get a note from the PTA president. The PTA is thinking about taking the board to a grand jury. I get a note from old Jerry, now *actually* back in the classroom—am I going to play the football pool again this year? The answers to all these are easy—I don't know, OK, go ahead, and yes.

School has started. The funny thing is that this time we are all a little sympathetic toward Him.

During the summer, and during the past three years, the district has been up against it about closing down schools. That is the modern thing to do. So we have had people from the California State Department of Education and various other experts too; we have had district committees, which include teachers and administrators and parents and everybody to deal with this problem. I have been on two of these committees myself. The problem? We got six thousand kids and fifteen schools.

Everyone, every committee, all the State Department of Education officials, agree that this won't do. You just can't have these little two-hundred-kid schools! Why not? Well, costs. Administrative, custodial, utilities . . . no. Have to close schools.

Well, we all got that, and the idea was to close three little elementary schools and make Spanish Main into a Middle School—so therefore He would have sixth graders here, making a bunch more kids, and then we could free up elective teachers, expand the program, and He was ecstatic, but . . .

But. But the board, confronted in public meetings by parents who did not want their little neighborhood schools closed, chickened out. They decided to forgo the advice of all those experts and committees. They didn't close any schools. Spanish Main can't, therefore, be a Middle School. He is out of business.

Our schedule is a mess. It is always a mess, with fifty-six kids in one social studies class and thirteen in the one next door. This year, it is the same, of course, but now we blame it on the board, not on Him. As time goes on, we'll blame it on Him again, but not right yet.

But I go down to my classroom. Room 33. Inside it, I close the door, and all of the above, most every concern brought up in this book, falls away.

I look around. There are thirty-five desks. They are all clean. The floor shines, having been worked on during the summer. I take a look at the darkening curtain. Well, no, still ripped, as it's been for ten years. How about the fountain? Well, again no, just drips out a drop.

I go around and open closet doors. The books are there, just as Andy put them. Printed maps, left over, are there. I remind myself to order more, right today.

Sitting there in this vacant room, looking out at the grass—one solitary black-and-white cat sits over a gopher hole, waiting—I am very content.

Why am I content? Well, I just am. I am like every other schoolteacher, I think. I am in this room, it is my room, it'll do, and, as I start to think about what I'll do this coming year, I realize, with much pleasure, that I know what I'm doing here.

I know what I'm going to do.

No kidding! Know what you're going to do? Given all the complications you've written about, the furor, the plans, the upsets, the wrongs, the problems, the idiocies, the state of the nation, the world. . . ? You know what to do?

Certainly. We all do. We teachers. We public-school teachers. We plan to teach school.

I admit that now, sitting here in Room 33, that maybe it is just now, this moment, that I take a look and regard myself as a schoolteacher. It's a description which is hard to avoid. I have worked here at Spanish Main since 1960. Every day, each year, since then. I know that when I write—I know that when I sit around and think or talk—that I have thought of myself as a musician or a fisherman or a ballplayer or, perhaps, just a man-about-town. Fact is, that I don't have to worry, really, about describing myself anymore. I teach school, in Spanish Main Junior High, to seventh graders. I have been a schoolteacher.

Now I sit here and think about social studies. I always teach social studies to seventh graders. I disapprove of the course. It does not work. Reading and language (which I always teach), I think to myself, well, they do work in a sense.

Seventh-grade social studies is supposed to be about ancient man, from cavemen, say, until Columbus—the works. Plus geography, principally that of the Middle East.

I myself have some interest in the subject. I know about Mr. Leakey. I love seeing Jane Goodall's film about the chimps. I've read and reread Konrad Lorenz. The kids do not seem, in seventh grade, to share this interest.

I'm going to figure it out this time, I tell myself. At the same time, I start to think about the school itself—it may be because I've just written all these pages about schools. I do take a look at it.

What in the world is so bad about this joint? I find myself saying. The rooms are big, roomy, we have this black-and-white cat outside. We have a good, big multiuse room where the kids eat lunch (many of them on our revisionist free lunch, of course). If they don't serve Spanish rice, they serve nachos.

If my curtain is ripped, the fact is we can still show Jane Goodall and the Chimps.

We have two huge art rooms. The people teaching *this* art know what they are doing, and they have paper, paints, clay, and pottery wheels and they can make prints and they have more stuff around for kids to use than the young Picasso ever had.

The library is right across from me. They have some twenty thousand volumes in it. We have had a series of smart librarians over the years and thus the library contains not only hundreds of kids' books but encyclopedias, magazines, big illustrated history books, wonderful biographies, every classic book ever written . . . a wealth of stuff is there.

The shops. Two great rooms, a hundred thousand dollars'

worth of equipment, smart guys who know how to operate it—you could build a house with this stuff, and we have guys who can show you how to do it, should you want to.

Two huge grassy fields.

Besides, in the library—it's modern times—we got cassette viewers and what-all. We've got computers, and we got computer teachers.

We have basketballs and baseballs and footballs and volleyballs and even soccer balls—an un-American sport of which I disapprove, but we have them. We have Gary, who played with Earl "The Pearl" Monroe, to teach these sports, plus Beth to teach dance or aerobics or whatever is called for in that line. We have tennis courts . . .

Of course, we have textbooks. My eye falls on the hateful seventh-grade social studies text, as I poke around in the closets. This book was the result of a teacher-admin committee, just as the book says. It is beneath contempt.

When I was in seventh grade, I tell myself, we had a book about Egypt by Breasted, a certified big-shot academic. The progressive movement was in charge. Now I have this text, this outrage, and I'm supposed to *use* it.

This book likes to tell about how Neanderthal man was a wonderful ecologist.

This book likes to talk about Egyptian culture, but fails to mention either hieroglyphics or embalming, let alone the Book of the Dead. Slaves were treated there, it points out, probably better than *some* people in *some* countries today.

The ancient Hebrews get some mention as land-use experts. The Old Testament is not brought up.

What do I want to do with this bloody social studies class? I begin to think about looking out the window and we'll see the cat there and envision fifteen or so of us, naked as jaybirds, looking around for something to eat (first of all, the kitty) and . . . well, I've done all that. *Concepts,* get across the idea that there was a time . . . and then there was a time . . . people learned how to grow their own food . . . settled down there in Ur or Jericho . . .

Whether or not we learned more from Breasted than these kids will from this? Well, at least we'll do geography. I can get maps. The atlases though, good, big paperback atlases, Hammond's *Historical Atlas*es, are about gone. I've had them some fifteen years, bought with Rabbit Mountain (alternative) money back then. The district's sixteen-million-dollar budget cannot afford fifty dollars' worth of atlases. We'll *make* another map then, a big, colored map and draw on it the principal rivers, the mountain ranges, the seas, locate the old towns, Carthage, Ur, Babylon, Alexandria, Troy, Samarkand . . . Knossos . . .

The year's lesson now planned, I can sit back and take it easy. We can trace Odysseus' voyage, we can . . .

Check the dictionaries. Plenty of new ones, but I prefer Thorndike's. Thorndike, another old progressive, tried to give definitions for words that the kid looking up the word might possibly be able to understand. The other dictionary defines "lust" as "a propensity to venery."

Of course, Thorndike's kids' dictionary doesn't bring up "lust" at all. What it does, though, is give derivations. I had a lot of fun with derivations myself in school, and so of course will force my students now to have a lot of fun with them too.

There are still thirty-three Thorndikes. With luck, that'll be enough for one more year.

You see? We, the teachers, know what to do.

I think about the school itself, again. No household, at least none in Tierra Firma, has got these books, these art materials, these basketballs, these grassy fields, these computers, this library, these maps, these Thorndikes. . . . And what about music? Haven't we got this great music room, haven't we got a great music teacher, haven't we got flutes and saxophones, both tenor and alto, clarinets, French horns, trumpets, trombones, haven't we got oboes? Guitars? Got them all, there for the taking and using? Haven't we got drums? Has any family in Tierra Firma got them all? And have they got a teacher? Have they got this sheet music? These music stands, or microphones?

Can you come here as a kid and learn anything? It looks to me as though you could come here as a twelve-year-old kid in the seventh grade and learn just about anything you wanted to learn. You could learn basketball, soccer, the classics, Spanish, geography, computers; how to play the oboe, learn to draw, paint, and use the potter's wheel; how to use the library; certainly learn to diagram sentences, take notes, write essays and book reports; you could read *Treasure Island* even if you didn't have it at home, *Little Women, The Diary of Anne Frank, Helen Keller*—we have this stuff, and we, the teachers, know about it and you can learn about all this and plenty else, right here.

We are good enough. The school is good enough. Mathematics? You can learn here to add and subtract if, somehow, you didn't get it before; we got people here who can teach you algebra should that be what you want or need to know. Geometry? Sure thing.

I poke around a bit more in the closets. I have, maybe, five hundred paperback books of all sorts. I see Howard Fast, I see *Chicano Cruz,* I see *Olympic Heroes,* I see *Johnny Wooden's Basketball Secrets,* I see *The Trojan War* and *Legends of Hercules,* and Poe's stories, including "The Pit and the Pendulum" . . .

I see a good stock of three-holed, blue-lined paper (the margin line is red) and of plain, white ditto paper for drawing maps (or for just drawing) or even for making dittos from about vocabulary and those derivations. I have masking tape, a stapler (and staples), marking pens, roll slips, and Progress Reports aplenty, and a listing of films from the County Film Library, which means that the county will deliver, once again weekly, *Jane Goodall, The Gold Bug, The Lottery,* and *Ishi in Two Worlds* at my request . . .

To go along with all this stuff, I have class lists of twelve-

and thirteen-year-olds who will come in this very room, like it or not, right after Labor Day. Two groups; one for reading and language, first and second periods. Twenty-eight kids—not so bad. Thirty-six for social studies, third period. Not so good. That is the top allowed in the contract, but you are supposed to begin with fewer, thirty-three, to allow for "emergencies." Emergencies are not supposed to come about on the first day. Well, some may not show up. The names, anyway, are three-quarters Hispanic but I know that many of these Spanish names will belong to Filipino kids, along with others named Madayag, Manansala, Madarang. Anh-Phuong Le, several Lees, some Wongs, two Japanese, a scattering of Johnsons and Martins and Richardses. I know, too, that a couple of the Hispanic boys will be *cholos* and wear earrings and shave their heads and wear hair-nets, out of a belief common in the San José barrio that their hair will thus grow out straight and look Indian instead of Mediterranean, but that otherwise these colorful groups will get along pretty well without any great racist divisions, these little kids having made, somehow, a great deal of progress along those lines in the last ten years or so without any of us—certainly not I—having any idea about how this was achieved . . . but I do know that *that,* specifically, is a part of this combat against ignorance, and superstition.

I look down the list for Samoans; things won't be exactly right without Samoan youth here. OK! Yeoman. *Yeoman!* Christian! I turn off the light, leave the room, lock the door. Lessons all planned for the year, my mind turns to *Mutiny on the Bounty* . . . I'll look in the faculty room, now, get coffee, see my colleagues, all armed with class lists, lessons planned, strategies mulled over, shiny classroom floors, clean desks, reams of three-holed, blue-lined paper . . .

So with all this stuff, these books, those films, basketballs, class lists, teachers, and so on, then why doesn't this school work?

It does work! I say.

Well, it don't work too good!

I begin the old arguments all over to myself. Now look, I say, if you really wanted to think up the worst possible situation in which to "learn" things, in which to concentrate on a problem or on a story, understand something like evolution, remember the name *Agamemnon,* the *worst possible* way to go about these things, then what you would do is get together some thirty twelve-year-olds and put them in a room together, just as, in fact, American public schools do now and have done forever and will go on doing . . .

Given that impossible situation, we, teachers, are here to combat ignorance and superstition, and we'll combat them. If we never win any outright victory, it is also clear that we can't lose, can't be totally defeated. Here the race is to the swift and the slow and those (most of us) in between. What we are going to do, all of us in there in Room 33 on Tuesday after Labor Day, is live our lives there, under certain circumstances, just as we will always do, in and out of school, either alone, reading *Mutiny on the Bounty,* or together with thirty others deciding whether to do our derivations or sabotage the fountain . . .

It works! I mutter to myself . . . just as being alive works . . .

Goddammit! A colleague is examining the bulletin board. I've got yard duty the first week! Morning duty too, the one I hate most of all, and He knows it!

It don't work too good! . . . yeah, but it. . . . No. Enough for now. . . .

Epilogue: Swan Song

In another summertime, I rented a beach house near the village of Bolinas, and each morning I took Jay and Jack down to fish for perch and shiners in the channel, play in the boats, roam the beach. I myself went up to spend some time in Smiley's Bar-and-Bait-Shop School.

The school itself, like all schools, had plenty of administrators, teachers, and professors. It had visiting scholars like myself. It had shaky professors emeritus, especially evident in the morning. A well-rounded curriculum was presented, from the life histories of the administration to the ingratitude of children, from the world-record rosetail perch (seven and one-quarter pound! said Harry the chancellor) to the possible hippie invasion of northern California (They ain't a hippie within a hundred mile of here! said Fred, a chief administrator).

The subject, this one morning that I remember—I seem to be at the stage where one says, remember clear as day—the subject was the decline of striped-bass fishing in the Bolinas channel. The channel was famous for that fishery each summer; in fact, none presently were being caught. Lectures were being given to explain it; pollution, sea lions, the A-bomb tests, pesticide, fluoridation.

Suddenly, one young man, a teaching assistant, one imagines, full of psychedelic screwdrivers, confronted us with the brilliant theory that no striped bass were being caught because no one was fishing for them! *No one,* he shouted, captivating us with his logic, was fishing because none were being caught! Since no one was fishing, he cried, had not been fishing for *two weeks,* we all assumed that there was no run of striped bass in the channel! How did we know? Sitting there in Smiley's Bar-and-Bait-Shop School, *how did we know* that there was not a *secret* striped-bass run going on in the channel, right now?

Well, Smiley's was a good school, I thought. After that lecture, most of us went off to keep office hours elsewhere. (And if there was no Smiley in sight, what did that matter? There was no George Washington or Benjamin Franklin in sight at most schools either.)

Still, the thing which really made Smiley's a good school was that there were no students. No *youth.* There were no kids. A benevolent government had made them illegal. The teachers were able, thus, to teach without disruption. The administration's rules were followed, lest one be eighty-sixed, or required to pay one's bar bill.

I think that it can be easily shown why youth, students, and kids detract from the Good School. For the one error made by the founders of Smiley's Bar-and-Bait-Shop School was to have created the bait shop. In the midst of the decline in striped bass, it still sold hooks, leaders, bait, sinkers, and line, to everyone. I recall when the school met its match—recall it clear as day—by the Coming of the Kid.

This one morning, only Chancellor Harry and I are present. Harry visibly needs time to get ready for the day. His hands seem to shake. He makes himself a screwdriver, and only then gets me my beer. I understand; Smiley's School holds Adult Education classes in the evening too. I personally never attend, but obviously it is a long, hard day for the top administration.

We sit. I have the sports page. Harry has his screwdriver and his head. Suddenly, Harry wheels around, looks out the blue-tinted window. He has heard something; I see that he suspects something is happening that no good school should have to endure!

He comes back to whisper to me, Oh, Lord have mercy, man, here comes the fucking kid!

The coming of a student, a kid, is at least troublesome for all schools. At most, it is a disaster. We can hear the Kid come in through the bait-shop door. The bait-shop counter comes just up to the half wall dividing the room, and so we can't see him. He is there though, waiting.

Harry's mouth pulls down in a spasm. I ask him, hurriedly, for another beer. He gives it to me, gratefully, but then draws himself up and marches with set face around the corner to the bait shop. Harry is courageous.

I listen. Nothing happens. Then I hear Harry say, You want something, Kid? The Kid mumbles. Then nothing. Then again, I hear Harry say, Well, if you make up yore mind you want something, you call me. I can't just stand here forever, you know!

Back in the bar, we wait. We both know that the Kid is still out there. I can *see* Harry's head hurting. I am in good shape; as a visiting professor, I don't have to deal with students. Still, we wonder, why can't the Kid come by at three in the afternoon instead of early in the morning, when all Harry wants is peace and quiet, aspirin, a drink, and time to think?

I decide to get out of here. But Harry gives us both a beer and then marches resolutely over to the bait shop. He is going to get it over with.

One hook, I can hear the Kid say. I imagine Harry sighing with relief. He can handle that one.

One hook? says Harry. Sure! I hear him rattling around

boxes of hooks and sinkers, lures. Here you are, Kid! Ten cents.

All I can hear is a mumble from the Kid.

What do you mean, you don't want that kind? Harry's voice is shrill. He's starting too soon, I know from experience. That's the only kind I got.

The Kid knows better. Kids always know better.

Yeah, well, oh those, says Harry. Them snelled hooks. Sure I got those, but they come six to a pack. Thirty cents!

Mumble.

Yeah, naw, but we don't sell just one of them! We only sell these others one at a time. You want one?

Mumble.

I listen. Chancellor Harry is too eager to get it over with. It's really tragic.

He goes on. Buy these hooks! Dime apiece! These are Eagle Claw hooks! Damn good hooks! I caught many a fish on them hooks!

M-m-m-m-m. The other guy . . . says the Kid.

Yeah, but I don't care about no other guy! What other guy? No, he didn't tell you that, either. Also, they ain't no other guy! Don't come in here and lie to me! Buy these snelled hooks by the pack, cheaper; you only got a dime, buy this one!

M-m-m-m-m; these other kind.

But I already told you! Look, you got thirty cents? Buy these!

Mumble.

Then buy this one for a dime! How come you need a hook anyway?

Oh, boy. I recognize that Harry has just lost. I had been in the same position many times. Never say to a student, How come? You are bound to lose.

Look, Kid, says Harry, you lost yore hook, you got it snagged on rocks and seaweed and mess and you gonna lose more hooks! Don't tell me you ain't! Look, Kid, what's it gonna be? I ain't got all day. I got work to do . . . look Kid, buy the one, I'll even tie it on for you, is that the problem? You don't know how to tie it on? Listen, Kid, I'm not gonna . . .

I have concentrated on the sports page, like any good teacher. Let this cup pass from me, I pray, and I read for the second time about the Giants' thrilling battle for fourth place. When I come to, Harry is back behind the bar.

How did it come out, Harry? I ask. I imply that, as a member of the staff, I have a right to know.

What? says Harry. Oh, you mean the Kid? Well, he left about five minutes ago.

Yeah, but what happened?

Harry would like to ignore this question. I understand that, but I need to know. With the hooks, Harry, I say.

Oh. Well, you heard the little bastard. Today it's one hook. Fine. But before it was one bait shrimp—you ever try to pry loose *one* shrimp from a pack of frozen shrimp?—and before that it was a piece of line *this long* off a thousand-yard spool of Dacron which he planned to buy for *one cent* and before that . . . Harry gets up and paces the length of the bar—hell, man, I can't stand there all day arguing with that little . . .

So what happened, Harry? I am inexorable.

And so, hell, I broke open the fucking pack of snelled hooks and gave him one! Jesus, if my head would just let up . . .

I say nothing, but I wait.

I'll throw his ass right out, next time! says Harry.

No doubt. Silence from me.

So I give him the snelled hook for a nickel!

Harry has returned to his seat, and looks out the blue window.

Give it to him for a nickel, and threw in a free one extra! And then he finally left!

. . .

That very evening I went out alone to the channel and walked the edge of the water, and about six, I saw the giant, brown pelicans wheeling and lurching through the air like kites and then, *wham!* or *blooie!* they dove or fell (if you've ever seen the beautiful pelicans' ungainly dive) and I unlimbered my rod and tied on my pretty feathered jig and cast it in a marvelous arc out into the channel where the pelicans were sitting or diving into the water, feeding. I knew that the pelicans were feeding on bait fish, and I knew that the secret striped bass were there, chasing those bait fish, and I knew that I was the only fisherman on the beach, and I knew that I had learned this from school.

I cast and cast into the glassy evening sea, into the glorious orange sunset, casting like a god, perfectly, without any backlash and without snagging the jig in kelp or rocks, bouncing the lure off those pelicans' backs time after time, causing pelican uproars, and I cast for an hour or so without any strike at all.

There were no secret striped bass in the channel.

ABOUT THE AUTHOR

James Herndon is the author of *The Way It Spozed to Be* and *How to Survive in Your Native Land*. He lives in California, where he has been a classroom teacher for more than twenty years. He is also the head of his local teacher's union.